Battleground
OPERATION MAR

NIJMEGEN

Battleground series:

Stamford Bridge & Hastings *by* Peter Marren
Wars of the Roses - Wakefield / Towton *by* Philip A. Haigh
Wars of the Roses - Barnet *by* David Clark
Wars of the Roses - Tewkesbury *by* Steven Goodchild
Wars of the Roses - The Battles of St Albans *by*
Peter Burley, Michael Elliott & Harvey Wilson
English Civil War - Naseby *by* Martin Marix Evans, Peter Burton
and Michael Westaway
English Civil War - Marston Moor *by* David Clark
War of the Spanish Succession - Blenheim 1704 *by* James Falkner
War of the Spanish Succession - Ramillies 1706 *by* James Falkner
Napoleonic - Hougoumont *by* Julian Paget and Derek Saunders
Napoleonic - Waterloo *by* Andrew Uffindell and Michael Corum
Zulu War - Isandlwana *by* Ian Knight and Ian Castle
Zulu War - Rorkes Drift *by* Ian Knight and Ian Castle
Boer War - The Relief of Ladysmith *by* Lewis Childs
Boer War - The Siege of Ladysmith *by* Lewis Childs
Boer War - Kimberley *by* Lewis Childs

Mons *by* Jack Horsfall and Nigel Cave
Néry *by* Patrick Tackle
Le Cateau *by* Nigel Cave and Jack Shelden
Walking the Salient *by* Paul Reed
Ypres - Sanctuary Wood and Hooge *by* Nigel Cave
Ypres - Hill 60 *by* Nigel Cave
Ypres - Messines Ridge *by* Peter Oldham
Ypres - Polygon Wood *by* Nigel Cave
Ypres - Passchendaele *by* Nigel Cave
Ypres - Airfields and Airmen *by* Mike O'Connor
Ypres - St Julien *by* Graham Keech
Ypres - Boesinghe *by* Stephen McGreal
Walking the Somme *by* Paul Reed
Somme - Gommecourt *by* Nigel Cave
Somme - Serre *by* Jack Horsfall & Nigel Cave
Somme - Beaumont Hamel *by* Nigel Cave
Somme - Thiepval *by* Michael Stedman
Somme - La Boisselle *by* Michael Stedman
Somme - Fricourt *by* Michael Stedman
Somme - Carnoy-Montauban *by* Graham Maddocks
Somme - Pozières *by* Graham Keech
Somme - Courcelette *by* Paul Reed
Somme - Boom Ravine *by* Trevor Pidgeon
Somme - Mametz Wood *by* Michael Renshaw
Somme - Delville Wood *by* Nigel Cave
Somme - Advance to Victory (North) 1918 *by* Michael Stedman
Somme - Flers *by* Trevor Pidgeon
Somme - Bazentin Ridge *by* Edward Hancock
Somme - Combles *by* Paul Reed
Somme - Beaucourt *by* Michael Renshaw
Somme - Redan Ridge *by* Michael Renshaw
Somme - Hamel *by* Peter Pedersen
Somme - Villers-Bretonneux *by* Peter Pedersen
Somme - Airfields and Airmen *by* Mike O'Connor
Airfields and Airmen of the Channel Coast *by* Mike O'Connor
In the Footsteps of the Red Baron *by* Mike O'Connor
Arras - Airfields and Airmen *by* Mike O'Connor
Arras - The Battle for Vimy Ridge *by* Jack Shelden & Nigel Cave
Arras - Vimy Ridge *by* Nigel Cave
Arras - Gavrelle *by* Trevor Tasker and Kyle Tallett
Arras - Oppy Wood *by* David Bilton
Arras - Bullecourt *by* Graham Keech
Arras - Monchy le Preux *by* Colin Fox
Walking Arras *by* Paul Reed
Hindenburg Line *by* Peter Oldham
Hindenburg Line - Epehy *by* Bill Mitchinson
Hindenburg Line - Riqueval *by* Bill Mitchinson
Hindenburg Line - Villers-Plouich *by* Bill Mitchinson
Hindenburg Line - Cambrai Right Hook *by* Jack Horsfall & Nigel Cave
Hindenburg Line - Cambrai Flesquières *by* Jack Horsfall & Nigel Cave
Hindenburg Line - Saint Quentin *by* Helen McPhail and Philip Guest

Hindenburg Line - Bourlon Wood *by* Jack Horsfall & Nigel Cave
Cambrai - Airfields and Airmen *by* Mike O'Connor
Aubers Ridge *by* Edward Hancock
La Bassée - Neuve Chapelle *by* Geoffrey Bridger
Loos - Hohenzollern Redoubt *by* Andrew Rawson
Loos - Hill 70 *by* Andrew Rawson
Fromelles *by* Peter Pedersen
The Battle of the Lys 1918 *by* Phil Tomaselli
Accrington Pals Trail *by* William Turner
Poets at War: Wilfred Owen *by* Helen McPhail and Philip Guest
Poets at War: Edmund Blunden *by* Helen McPhail and Philip Guest
Poets at War: Graves & Sassoon *by* Helen McPhail and Philip Guest
Gallipoli *by* Nigel Steel
Gallipoli - Gully Ravine *by* Stephen Chambers
Gallipoli - Anzac Landing *by* Stephen Chambers
Gallipoli - Landings at Helles *by* Huw & Jill Rodge
Walking the Italian Front *by* Francis Mackay
Italy - Asiago *by* Francis Mackay
Verdun: Fort Douaumont *by* Christina Holstein
Walking Verdun *by* Christina Holstein
Zeebrugge & Ostend Raids 1918 *by* Stephen McGreal

Germans at Beaumont Hamel *by* Jack Sheldon
Germans at Thiepval *by* Jack Sheldon

SECOND WORLD WAR

Dunkirk *by* Patrick Wilson
Calais *by* Jon Cooksey
Boulogne *by* Jon Cooksey
Saint-Nazaire *by* James Dorrian
Normandy - Pegasus Bridge *by* Carl Shilleto
Normandy - Merville Battery *by* Carl Shilleto
Normandy - Utah Beach *by* Carl Shilleto
Normandy - Omaha Beach *by* Tim Kilvert-Jones
Normandy - Gold Beach *by* Christopher Dunphie & Garry Johnson
Normandy - Gold Beach Jig *by* Tim Saunders
Normandy - Juno Beach *by* Tim Saunders
Normandy - Sword Beach *by* Tim Kilvert-Jones
Normandy - Operation Bluecoat *by* Ian Daglish
Normandy - Operation Goodwood *by* Ian Daglish
Normandy - Epsom *by* Tim Saunders
Normandy - Hill 112 *by* Tim Saunders
Normandy - Mont Pinçon *by* Eric Hunt
Normandy - Cherbourg *by* Andrew Rawson
Normandy - Commandos & Rangers on D-Day *by* Tim Saunders
Das Reich - Drive to Normandy *by* Philip Vickers
Oradour *by* Philip Beck
Market Garden - Nijmegen *by* Tim Saunders
Market Garden - Hell's Highway *by* Tim Saunders
Market Garden - Arnhem, Oosterbeek *by* Frank Steer
Market Garden - Arnhem, The Bridge *by* Frank Steer
Market Garden - The Island *by* Tim Saunders
Rhine Crossing – US 9th Army & 17th US Airborne *by* Andrew Raws
British Rhine Crossing – Operation Varsity *by* Tim Saunders
British Rhine Crossing – Operation Plunder *by* Tim Saunders
Battle of the Bulge – St Vith *by* Michael Tolhurst
Battle of the Bulge – Bastogne *by* Michael Tolhurst
Channel Islands *by* George Forty
Walcheren *by* Andrew Rawson
Remagen Bridge *by* Andrew Rawson
Cassino *by* Ian Blackwell
Anzio *by* Ian Blackwell
Dieppe *by* Tim Saunders
Fort Eben Emael *by* Tim Saunders
Crete – The Airborne Invasion *by* Tim Saunders
Malta *by* Paul Williams

Battleground Europe
OPERATION MARKET GARDEN

NIJMEGEN
GRAVE AND GROESBEEK

Tim Saunders

LEO COOPER

*To my son Jamie Saunders
with love*

Published by
Pen & Sword Books Limited
47 Church Street, Barnsley, South Yorkshire S70 2AS
Copyright © Tim Saunders 2001, 2011

ISBN 978-0-85052-798-8

A CIP record of this book is available
from the British Library

Printed in the United Kingdom by
CPI UK

*For up-to-date information on other titles produced under the Leo Cooper
imprint, please telephone or write to:*

Pen & Sword Books Ltd, FREEPOST SF5, 47 Church Street
Barnsley, South Yorkshire S70 2BR
Telephone 01226 734555

CONTENTS

21 September 1944
British tanks crossing
Nijmegen Bridge to
continue the battle. A
welcoming party of
relieved American 82nd
Division ('All American')
paratroopers awaited
them at the other side.

INTRODUCTION

As a British soldier my interest in MARKET GARDEN as a whole, rather than just the Arnhem battle, was born out of an incident at the Oosterbeek CWGC cemetery on the fiftieth anniversary. While accompanying a group of Dorset Regiment veterans, red-bereted veterans called out 'Ah, XXX Corps. On time for a change!' and other such comments. At first, this seemed to me to be normal banter and friendly rivalry between soldiers of different units but an uncomfortable tension grew between the two groups of veterans. Clearly, after fifty years, feelings of resentment at the defeat and virtual destruction of 1st Airborne Division still ran deep. The Dorsets, who were commemorating their comrades who died crossing the Rhine to join the Paras, knew that they had failed to reach Oosterbeek in time or in sufficient strength to make a difference. However, they also knew that they had fought all the way from Normandy and had done their best. Nor could they, even former company commanders, account for MARKET GARDEN's failure.

I quickly discovered that there was a lack of detailed information on the part played by the US Airborne Divisions available in the UK. Even, Geoffrey Powell's excellent book, *The Devils Birthday, Bridges to Arnhem 1944* covers the Arnhem battle, in which he fought, in considerably more detail than those at Grave, Groesbeek and Nijmegen. Even in the States, the number of books, on what was regarded by the 82nd Airborne as their most difficult battle of the war, in no way compares with the number of those concentrating on Arnhem. In the case of XXX Corps, a short history was written, complementing General Horrocks's book *Corps Commander,* but to piece together a detailed account, I have had to resort to divisional and regimental histories. In these, events are covered in more or less detail, with often imprecise information on what was going on elsewhere on the battlefield. Colonel Robert Kershaw's book, *It Never Snows in September,* covers the German perspective of MARKET GARDEN. However, as a Parachute Regiment officer, he too understandably concentrates on Arnhem.

Why is there this disparity? The successful fight for the Nijmegen Bridge was every bit as desperate as that fought by 1

6

The Nijmegen road bridge with the rail bridge behind. The city is to the left of the picture and Arnhem is just ten miles across the river to the north.

Para Brigade to reach the Arnhem bridge on 18 September 1944. The reason is simple; the correspondents who landed with 1st British Airborne Division were able to file vivid pieces to their editors that made compelling reading and caught the imagination of readers on both sides of the Atlantic. Also, few who have heard a recording of Stanley Maxted's BBC report can not have been affected by the dramatic events he captured. On the other hand, only two correspondents were accredited to each of the US airborne divisions and in the case of the 82nd Airborne they received no help in filing their stories. At the time, the almost total lack of comment on the US part in the battle has led to lack of knowledge and understanding of the MARKET GARDEN campaign as a whole. This as General Brereton, Commander First Allied Airborne Army, predicted has had an enduring effect:

'In the years to come everyone will remember Arnhem, but no one will remember that two American divisions fought their hearts out in the Dutch canal country and whipped hell out of the Germans.'

This book seeks to bring together little known, out of print and archive material into an account covering the 82nd Airborne

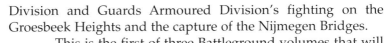

Division and Guards Armoured Division's fighting on the Groesbeek Heights and the capture of the Nijmegen Bridges.

This is the first of three Battleground volumes that will cover all sixty-four miles of XXX Corps's route from Joe's Bridge on the Escaut Canal to Arnhem on the Rhine. Another volume will cover the Guards Armoured Division's capture and breakout from Joe's Bridge onto *Hell's Highway*, which was held by the paratroopers of 101st Airborne. The third volume will cover the battles fought on the polder land of *The Island* by 43rd Wessex Division in their attempt to reach 1st Airborne Division at Arnhem and that division's evacuation from Oosterbeek. The fighting at Arnhem itself will be the subject of two further books in the *Battleground* series.   Enjoy the tour.

Tim Saunders
Lichfield, Staffs

ACKNOWLEDGMENTS

I am indebted to veterans on both sides of the Atlantic for their help and advice in writing this book. There was not much *Battleground* style material readily available on the Grave, Groesbeek and Nijmegen areas of the North West European Campaign but veterans' contributions have helped fill this gap. Again, hard pressed staff from the regimental headquarters of the British units, whose fighting is covered by this book, have been most helpful; be they overworked regimental secretaries or highly knowledgeable volunteers. In America, veterans associations have helped me locate members who had tales to tell. Visits to the Public Record Office and airborne museums in Britain and Holland to view their archives were essential and I thank the staff unreservedly for their help.

It would be invidious to list by name all the Dutch people from the Nijmegen and Groesbeek area who have helped me in so many ways. Their help ranged from locating the more obscure sites to the provision of maps and photographs. However, their greatest contribution was their encouragement, warmth and friendliness. With many *ad hoc* German formations and units taking part in the fighting at Nijmegen, it has been difficult to make contact with former German soldiers. However, one particular divisional association has been of considerable help in clearing up some of Nijmegen's MARKET GARDEN myths.

Finally, I will again thank my family for their extremely tolerant support of this project and encouragement. I am also most grateful for the hours they have spent reading through the draft manuscript spotting my errors and inconsistencies. I am particularly grateful to my father-in-law Lieutenant Colonel Geoff Hill (Royal Engineers) for his sound military advice. Thank you one and all.

ADVICE TO VISITORS

Travel to Holland

There is currently a range of ferry crossings to mainland Europe and Holland from various UK ports that can be used by those visiting the MARKET GARDEN battlefields. In the north, Newcastle has an overnight service (fourteen hours) to Amsterdam and further south Hull has a similar service to Zeebrugge (Belgium). Harwich has sailings to the Hook of Holland (three and a half hours). Both Amsterdam and the Hook are about two hours drive from Nijmegen on good motorways. However, sailings from the East Coast are not as frequent and can be more costly than those from the Channel Ports but savings in fuel and tiredness always make these services worth considering. The Channel crossing, though shorter and quicker does mean that the visitor is faced with a four-hour drive from Calais, via busy motorways (toll-free) around Antwerp and through southern Holland. For those who dislike ferries there is the Channel Tunnel, but this option, though quicker, can be more expensive. It is worth checking out all the options available and make your selection of routes based on UK travel, ferry times and cost. Special offers and Internet deals are always worth keeping an eye open for and have, in my case, resulted in impromptu visits to the continental battlefields.

Traffic law requires you to carry a full driving licence, your vehicle registration document, warning triangle and a spare fuel can of an approved type. You should also take spare head light bulbs etc and, if your headlights do not have left hand drive adapters, black tape. Do not forget your passport and a GB sticker.

For those travelling by air and hiring cars, Amsterdam/Schipol is a major international hub while Eindhoven is a significant regional airport within an hour of Nijmegen. A good web site to visit for up to date travel information is:

http://www.visitholland.com/geninfo/travel/

Insurance

It is important to check that you are properly insured to travel to France, Belgium, Holland and Germany (the tour crosses the border briefly at Wyler). Firstly, check with your insurance broker to ensure that your car is properly covered for driving in the above countries and, secondly, make sure you have health cover. Form E111, available from main post offices and grants the bearer reciprocal treatment rights in most European countries but, even so, the visitor should consider

purchasing a package of travel insurance from a broker or travel agent. It is a legal requirement for a driver to carry a valid certificate of motor insurance.

Accommodation

As a Dutch holiday area, there are plenty of hotels and B and Bs in the Groesbeek area from which to chose. However, the area is very popular with walkers and, therefore, cheap accommodation, on occasions, can be difficult to find during the period Easter to October. Other hotels in the Nijmegen area cater for business customers and nearly always have space, particularly at weekends. There are a number of well-run campsites in the Groesbeek area. Information on availability of rooms and bookings can be made by telephone to the Groesbeek Tourist Office, whose staff all speak excellent English. A similar service is offered by the Nijmegen office. For those with access to the Internet a visit to the following web site will be helpful if searching for the better hotels, http:/hotels.bookings.nl/ tourist.nederland.hotbot.html/. A few hotels that feature in the following chapters are still open for business today. These include the Hotel Restaurant Sionshof half way between Groesbeek and the centre of Nijmegen. The Sionshof has a memorial to the 82nd Airborne Division on its walls and is where the Coldstream Guards were located during their period as divisional reserve.

Courtesy

Much of the Groesbeek area is open farmland. However, many of the surrounding villages were also a part of the battlefield and, consequently, heavily fought over. Please respect private property in both open country and villages, particularly avoiding driving on farm tracks and entering non-public areas in villages. Adequate views of the scene of the action can be enjoyed from public land. In the city of Nijmegen, drive carefully and please be careful not to block access by careless car parking. Although there are not as many cyclists on the Groesbeek Heights as elsewhere in flatter parts of Holland, please watch out for them and do not block cycle lanes. Do not be tempted to gain access to the bank of the Waal on the Nijmegen side without permission, as this is industrial private property. However, on the opposite side it is possible to walk down to the landing site. The people of Holland extend a genuine welcome to those who come to honour the memory of their Allied liberators. To preserve this welcome, please be courteous to the local people at all times.

Maps

Good maps are an essential prerequisite to a successful battlefield visit. Best of all is a combination of contemporary and modern maps. The *Battleground* series of course, provides a variety of maps. However, a full map sheet enables the visitor or indeed those who are exploring the battlefield from the comfort of their armchair, to put the battle in a wider context. A number of modern of maps are available in both the UK and Holland. A good road map of Holland and a city map of Nijmegen are essential to navigate the tour, most of the latter, however, do not cover Groesbeek area. This is best covered by a detailed map available in stationers and in garages in Nijmegen. Normally, detailed maps of the Netherlands are only available on order from a specialist map shop in the UK or as a special order through high street book shops such as Waterstones.

NCOs of the 82nd Airborne collect maps and ammunition at their departure airfields.

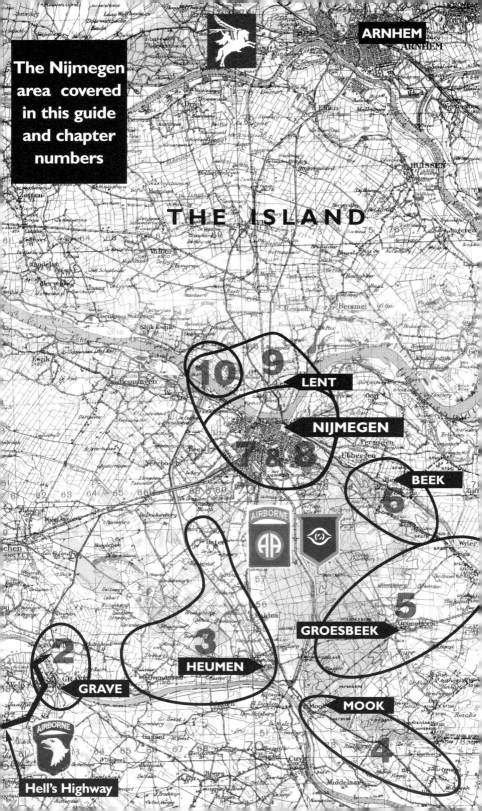

The Nijmegen area covered in this guide and chapter numbers

ARNHEM

THE ISLAND

10

9

LENT

NIJMEGEN

7 & 8

BEEK

6

AIRBORNE

AA

5

GROESBEEK

3

HEUMEN

2

GRAVE

MOOK

4

Hell's Highway

CHAPTER ONE

BACKGROUND AND THE MARKET GARDEN PLAN

'Had the pious teetotalling Monty wobbled into SHAEF with a hangover, I could not have been more astonished than I was by the daring adventure he proposed!'
General Omar Bradley.

It is not within the scope of this book to give a detailed analysis of the controversial background to Operation MARKET GARDEN. What follows, is a distillation of the political and military factors that shaped the plan in sufficient detail for the operation to be clearly set within the context of the North West European Campaign as a whole.

After D Day, the Allies initially made slow progress in terms of captured terrain, with the rate of progress, measured against Supreme Headquarters Allied Expeditionary Force (SHAEF) planners' expectations not being met. However, by mid-August, after some hard fighting, the Germans collapsed into defeat. The Normandy campaign was won and the German defeat, when it came, was as complete as was Montgomery's victory over his many critics. The remnants of the German Seventh Army, who

The sure sign of German defeat in Normandy – a road crammed with destroyed men and equipment.

had escaped destruction in the Falaise Pocket, streamed eastwards. The Germans made successive attempts to halt the Allies on the Seine (reached fifteen days ahead of Montgomery's target) and, subsequently, on the River Somme and any other topographic feature of tactical significance. However, the Allied armoured divisions' momentum was such that each obstacle was *'bounced'* and the advance continued, at rates of up to fifty miles per day. The lack of opposition and the Allies' reception as liberators, led to a feeling that the war was almost at an end. The contrast between the hard slogging of the Normandy battles and the swift advances, served only to sharpen in the minds of both commanders and front-line soldiers, the prospect of an early end to the war. The reader should judge the MARKET GARDEN plans against the contemporary, and seemingly reasonable, expectations of victory in Europe before the end of 1944.

Alliance Politics

General Dwight D Eisenhower took over conduct of the campaign from the newly promoted Field Marshal Montgomery on 1st September 1944. The extent of the Allied victory and the speed of the advance eastwards eclipsed SHAEF's ability to plan and led to Eisenhower not having a detailed military strategy to follow when he took full command. Eisenhower has been criticised for not being a decisive commander but, after Normandy, there was no shortage of plans being put forward by his generals. At one stage, it seemed as if he was agreeing to support all of them. However, Eisenhower's problems in selecting a strategy following the German collapse, became even more difficult, as national pride and his generals' personal ambitions became pre-eminent. In short, British and American plans were no longer subordinated to the common goal of defeating a powerful enemy. With such notoriously difficult characters as Patton and Montgomery to deal with, along with their respective press corps, Eisenhower's command was never going to be easy. In what at the time was the most frankly reported campaign of the Twentieth Century, the Supreme Commander was working primarily at a political level. Whatever the arguments in favour of Montgomery's narrow front advance into Germany, it would never have been politically acceptable to US public opinion to have Patton's

Montgomery was a notoriously difficult subordinate. This photograph of Montgomery and Eisenhower together illustrates, through body language and expressions, the problem between the two commanders.

Third Army halted, with the victor's laurels going to Montgomery. It is clear that Eisenhower found considerable favour with the arguments for the northern route to Berlin but political realities forced him to adopt the 'attack everywhere' philosophy that underpinned the US broad front strategy of the day.

Other than his generals' prestige and national pride, Eisenhower had other pressing political factors to consider as he came to his decisions on Sunday 7 September 1944. Firstly, there was the fact that after five years of war, Britain was at the end of her resources and, ideally, the war in Europe needed to be over by Christmas 1944. Secondly, V2 ballistic missiles, launched from north-west Holland, were falling on London. The need to clear the enemy from the area of the launch sites and thus take the missiles out of range, was one of Churchill's key requirements. Thirdly, another purely European factor was that the Prime Minister did not want a Soviet presence in the heart of Europe and, therefore, gaining as much territory and being the first to Berlin was important. Fourthly, the Ruhr industrial area, despite the Strategic Bomber Offensive was still the power house of Germany and in 1944 tank production actually rose to a record 19,002 vehicles. It was estimated that capturing the Ruhr Triangle would end the war within three months. All these factors had to be considered and balanced as the Supreme Commander made his decisions.

The fact that the Supreme Commander pleased none of his 'difficult' subordinate commanders, is illustrated by Patton's comment that Eisenhower was 'the best general the British have'. This indicates that he was at least even-handed. Another prophetic quote from Patton in 1944 summed up Eisenhower's role in the European campaign; 'he'd make a better president that a general'.

Logistics

Logistics lay at the route of Eisenhower's political and military problems: in early September, he could not sustain all or even a half of his forces in offensive operations at any one time. The rapid advance eastward led to his armies, still without a major port, being largely supplied through the artificial Mulberry harbour and across the Normandy beaches. Two hundred and fifty miles forward of their supply bases, commanders were prepared to lobby hard, in competition for all the supplies that they could get. Typically, they would paint an over-optimistic picture of the prospects on their front in order to secure additional resources: General Patton is widely acknowledged as the master of this technique.

However, the further the front advanced eastwards, the fewer troops were able to pursue the Germans. Infantry divisions were *'grounded'* and their trucks stripped from them to transport combat supplies needed to keep the armoured divisions mobile. Fewer troops at the front meant a reduction in combat power and at, the same time, they were having to cover wider frontages. Consequently, there was an increasing likelihood of an *ad hoc* German defence assembling sufficient force to halt the advancing Allies. To make the situation worse, it should also be borne in mind, that Allied soldiers were,

The shoulder patch worn by staff of HQ 1st Allied Airborne Army.

18

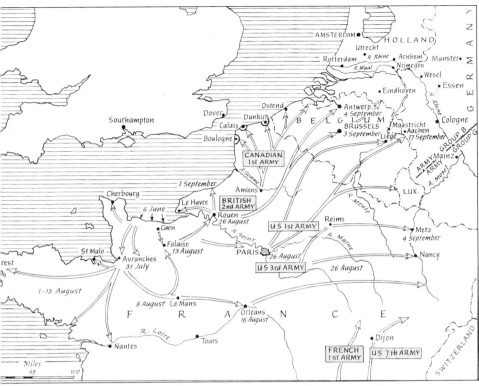

The general situation in North West Europe by September 1944.

understandably, increasingly unlikely to risk their lives in what they perceived to be the final weeks of the war.

First Allied Airborne Army

Airborne forces had been embraced by the US Army prior to the war and, following their successful use by the Germans in 1940, the British formed their first airborne units in 1940. By 1944 airborne forces were sufficiently strong to warrant grouping into their own Army, with a headquarters to look after their interests and advance their cause. Considerable resources, as strategic bomber commanders saw it, had been diverted into transport aircraft to support the new arm. The First Allied Airborne Army was also Eisenhower's only strategic reserve, contrary to the impression that the Germans still held as a result of the OVERLORD deception operation; FORTITUDE. In addition, the US Chief of Staff, General Marshall, was pressurising Eisenhower to find a use for this expensive asset, as the airborne divisions were *'coins burning holes in SHAEF's pocket'*. Attempts had been made to utilise 1st (British) Airborne Division but the speed of the ground advance had, frustratingly, eclipsed all plans for its use. However, as the armies in France and now Belgium began to lose momentum an opportunity for their use presented its-self. Eisenhower could easily support Montgomery's plan to enhance an earlier divisional plan (Operation COMET) to a corps level airborne operation, as Bradley was far from keen on airborne forces. He and other main US commanders would have preferred to have the air transports used in the logistic effort to support his armies. The allocation of an airborne corps to Twenty First Army Group was a way of satisfying the demands of both Montgomery and the Pentagon. However, would there be sufficient combat supplies available to support full execution of the plan? In short no. Alliance politics prevailed over pure military interest.

Intelligence

Not only were the impressions of soldiers at the front shaped by lack of opposition and the speed of advance but even normally reserved staff officers were optimistic that the war's end was near. As early as mid August, SHAEF's Intelligence Summary declared:

'Two and a half months of bitter fighting, culminating for the Germans in a blood-bath big enough even for their extravagant tastes, have brought the end of the war in Europe within sight, almost within reach.'

All indicators were that the German collapse was total. Tens of thousands of German soldiers were, in many cases, isolated or almost cut-off, in the fortified ports of France and the Low Countries. In addition, in early September 1944, the *Volksarmies* that were later to confront the Allies in the Ardennes and, during early 1945, on the Rhine, did not yet exist.

During early stages of planning for Operation COMET, some remarkably accurate intelligence that painted a less rosy picture, was received on 7 September 1944:

'... it is reported that one of the broken panzer divisions has been sent back to the area north of Arnhem to rest and refit; this might produce some 50 tanks.'

This was the Resistance passing on details of the arrival of the leading elements of the shattered II SS Panzer Corps (9th and 10th SS Panzer Divisions) from France to refit north of the

Rhine. The report continues:

'To-day's photographs together with ground reports from Dutch sources, indicate that the main direction of German movement is NW to SE; not only has 347 Div come down, but many of the SS training units which were near AMSTERDAM are now quartered in the excellent barracks at NIJMEGEN. There seems little doubt that our operational area will contain a fair quota of Germans, and the previous estimate of one division may prove to be not far from the mark; moreover it would not be surprising to find the high ground south of NIJMEGEN, Pt 83 the highest point in Holland - protected as it is by the MAAS - WAAL Canal to the west, the MAAS to the south, and the WAAL to the north, and guarding a vulnerable outpost of the Fatherland's frontier has been made into a hedgehog defensive position ...'

Major Brian Urquhart, Dorset Regiment, warned of the presence of panzers around Arnhem and was promptly sent on leave.

This is an early recognition of the dominating nature of the Groesbeek Heights. In MARKET GARDEN this area had to be seized and held by 82nd Airborne Division, if ground troops were to reach Arnhem. In the optimism of the time, the presence of a shattered panzer division and numerous *ad hoc* units did not seem to count as a significant planning factor, although some junior commanders had reservations about their missions. As recounted by Geoffrey Powell:

'At one battalion briefing, a company commander, on hearing the task allocated to a colleague, had leaned over to him and whispered "That should provide you with either a Victoria Cross or a wooden one".'

This tendency to ignore the enemy is highlighted by, Polish airborne commander, General Sosabowski's outburst 'But the Germans, General, the Germans'. Ignoring the enemy became even more marked as planning for MARKET GARDEN got under way. A little more than a week later, the intelligence

Polish General Sosabowski was uninpressed by the Airborne Plan.

planning documentation for the larger, corps scale, operation failed to mention most of the enemy positions and movements outlined above and ignored the significance of much more material. Accusations of ignoring intelligence, as it stood in the way of the conceived plan (cognitive dissonance), have been levelled against Montgomery and 1st Airborne Division in particular. Colonel Michael Hickey provides one explanation:

'Monty was very competitive. He wanted, as a battalion commander, his battalion to win all the trophies available in the Egyptian Command in the 1930s, and they probably did He competed against other generals, particularly in north-west Europe with General Patton, with whom his relationship was a pretty unstable one. They couldn't make each other out as men, because they were so radically different from each other: Patton the dashing, swashbuckling Southern cavalryman in the American army, Monty the ascetic, non-smoking, non swearing, non-drinking Cromwellian. And the competition grew to a head as the Allies broke out of the Normandy pocket and made their bid to go for the German border in the high summer and early autumn of 1944.'

Lieutenant General 'Boy' Browning.

The MARKET GARDEN Plan – Outline

Montgomery left his meeting with Eisenhower at Brussels on 7 September, with the resources of the Allied Airborne Army at his disposal and correctly or incorrectly believing that he had been promised *'absolute priority'* for logistics. His MARKET GARDEN plan, which he personally detailed down as far as divisional tasks, was delivered to General Miles Dempsey, Commander Second British Army on 10 September. It was a bold plan. Lieutenant General 'Boy' Browning was to command a corps of three airborne divisions, made up of 1st British Airborne Division, and 82nd and 101st US Airborne Divisions. Montgomery explained that the Airborne Corps, in Operation MARKET, was to seize important points (mainly rivers and canals) across Holland on an axis from the bridgehead on the Escaut Canal through

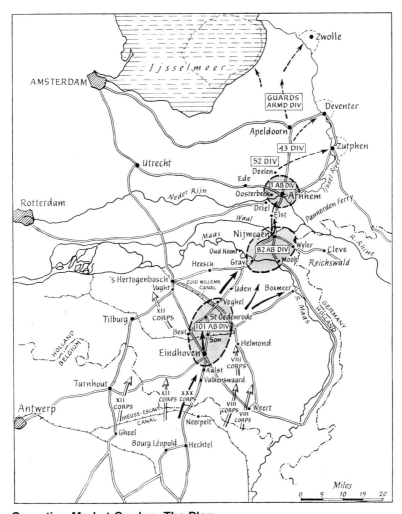

Operation Market Garden: The Plan.

Eindhoven, Nijmegen and Arnhem. Across this *'Carpet'* of airborne troops, in the GARDEN part of the operation, an armoured spearhead would drive north to the Zuyder Zee, some one hundred miles into enemy territory. From here, having outflanked the West Wall and cut-off hundreds of thousands of Germans in western Holland, the armoured forces would envelop the Ruhr and prepare to strike towards Berlin. Not only was General Bradley surprised at Montgomery's boldness but he also said *'Monty's plan was one of the most imaginative of the war.'*

It certainly was a bold plan but the whole concept was

German prisoners taken at Nijmegen demonstrate the extreme age-range of the troops being put into the field after the defeat in Normandy.

predicated on the fact that the German defences were a thin crust and that a properly concentrated and well-supported ground force could pierce it and reach the airborne divisions. Montgomery, as we shall see, successfully broke through the German defences on the Escaut Canal but what had not been envisaged was the escape of 82,000 soldiers of the German Fifteenth Army across the mouth of the Scheldt. Nor had it been anticipated that the shattered divisions from France, the North Sea coast and the 'ageing gentlemen of Germany's last reserves', would be able to form an effective defence.

General Lewis Brereton, commanding the Allied Airborne Army, had to bring two elements together in his plan. Firstly, there were the ground troops, represented by the headquarters of the Airborne Corps under Lieutenant General Browning and, secondly his fellow British and American airmen. The plan he developed gave primacy to the airforces' considerations, which did much to contribute to MARKET GARDEN's overall failure. The first decision was a daylight drop. With inexperienced aircrews and a moonless period, a repeat of the badly dispersed drops that opened D Day three months earlier was to be avoided. In addition, Brereton's aircraft were capable of flying less than

24

half of the Airborne Corps in one lift. A lack of ground crew compounded the problem and led to Major General Williams' USAAF IX Troop Carrier Command (TCC), recommending to Brereton that there should be only one lift per day. Thus, the airborne divisions were not going to arrive in a single 'clap of thunder' but over a period of three days. Worse still, in most cases, only half of the first lift would be available to seize objectives on the first day, as vital units had to defend Drop Zones (DZs) and Landing Zones (LZs) for subsequent lifts. Finally, as with Normandy, the airmen warned of heavy aircraft losses to flak. With the end of the war in sight, there was a general wish to avoid unnecessary casualties and senior air officers wishes prevailed. Consequently, DZs were to be sited away from flak positions and, therefore, well away from the ground troops' objectives. Crucially, Major General Urquhart had his request for a glider *coup de main* at the Arnhem Bridge turned down. However, even General Gavin (82nd Airborne), arguably MARKET GARDEN's most experienced Allied airborne commander, also eventually lost out to IX TCC's insistence that a *coup de main* on the Nijmegen Bridge was too dangerous. The landing serials at the northern end of the Nijmegen Road Bridge were eventually written out of the early drafts of IX TCC's plan on 16 September 1944. Only a parachute *coup de main* against the lightly defended Grave Bridge was allowed to go ahead. The over cautious approach of the air force commanders concerning the first lift, based on an understandable desire to avoid casualties, led to a far greater sacrifice by the aircrews

General Lewis Brereton, commander 1st Allied Airborne Army.

Troop Carrier Command badge incorperating a parachute and a glider.

25

over subsequent days.

General Browning had severe reservations about MARKET GARDEN, as illustrated by his famous off the cuff remark to Montgomery 'I think we may be going a bridge too far' but he was overruled. Having previously offered his resignation over what he saw a Brereton's disregard for ground elements of an earlier operation, he was in no position to influence the plan by repeating his threat. In addition, Major General Urquhart, although he was commanding the most exposed division, lacked airborne experience and, consequently, credibility to convince the airmen to change their plans.

In advance of the air armada, the Allied airforces were to fly 1,395 bomber and 1,240 fighter or fighter bomber sorties over southern Holland and the areas where the Airborne Corps were to drop. As a result of these attacks, the transports, paratroops and gliders were able to carry out the first phase of the operation with minimal losses. The P-51 Mustangs and P-47 Thunderbolts protecting the slow moving columns of transport aircraft had little to do. On the ground in the Groesbeek/ Nijmegen area, known troop concentrations in barracks and anti-aircraft positions were repeatedly attacked spoiling the gentle rear-area Sunday routine.

82nd Airborne Division's Mission and Plan

Faced with a far from ideal airborne plan, the 82nd Airborne Division's new commander faced a difficult problem. Brigadier

General Gavin briefing his staff and commanders.

American paratroopers load a trailer onto a Waco glider.

General James M Gavin or 'Slim Jim' as he was known to his troopers, was a tall, lean and tough ex-ranker who had led 505th Parachute Infantry Regiment (PIR) in action in the Mediterranean. In the UK for OVERLORD planning, he joined Eisenhower as his airborne advisor and during the Normandy battles acted as the 82nd's Assistant Divisional commander. On the Division's return to UK, at the age of thirty-seven, Gavin took over command of the 82nd Airborne and in doing so, became the US Army's youngest divisional commander of World War Two. General Gavin has described his mission in the Nijmegen area and some of the difficulties he envisaged that his division would have to deal with:

'The mission assigned to the 82nd Airborne Division was to seize the long bridge over the Mass River at Grave, to seize and hold the high ground in the vicinity of Groesbeek, to seize at least one of the four bridges over the Maas-Waal Canal, and finally to seize the big bridge at the city of Nijmegen. ... For my part, I was

27

General James Gavin prepares for the drop.

concerned about the very widespread dispersal that would take place in the initial landing. Inevitably, there would be huge gaps in the perimeter that I was to seize and defend, and some very difficult decisions had to be made concerning where the landings were to take place. We had learned from the very beginning in Sicily, that it is better to land near an objective and take heavy losses rather than have to fight on the ground to get it. On the other hand, we had so many objectives over such an extensive area - approximately twenty-five miles - that a complete loss of control of the division might take place the very moment the landings occurred if judgement was not exercised in allocating troops to particular objectives.'

In contrast to XXX Corps and 101st Airborne Division who had to fight through the enemy's forward positions in the newly formed German 1st *Fallschirmjäger* Army's Forward Combat Zone, the 82nd was to drop in the enemy's Rear Combat Zone. Here the 82nd should only encounter lines of communication troops and broken formations but this rosy prospect was to underestimate the German's capacity to find troops with which to mount an effective response. The MARKET GARDEN plan placed the 82nd's DZs in close proximity to the boundaries of the Netherlands Military District and *Weherkreis* VI (a military district in Germany) where several training schools and numerous rear echelon units were to be found. The latter were often made up of previously wounded, young or old soldiers or otherwise 'low quality' troops. An example would be units consisting entirely of soldiers who were hard of hearing or suffering from stomach problems. In addition, the 82nd were aware of and had recognised the importance of the presence of armoured divisions reportedly refitting in the Reichswald. In the event, these enemy tanks proved to be the remnants of II SS Panzer Corps who 1st Airborne Division encountered to the north-east of Arnhem; having been correctly assessed at twenty percent of its establishment. The Germans' genius in fighting with reportedly 'ineffective' or *ad hoc* formations was to test the widely dispersed American paratroopers in the days to come.

General Gavin's airlift on Sunday 17 September 1944 was only sufficient to drop his three parachute infantry regiments, a single battalion of artillery and deliver by glider, a limited portion of his divisional troops. They were to secure the various bridges, the DZs / LZs and to capture one or both of the

Nijmegen road and rail bridges. The denial of gliders to seize the Nijmegen Road Bridge must have been a cruel blow and a severe limiting factor. Meanwhile, 504 PIR was to drop on to DZs Easy and Oscar, located in the triangle between the River Maas and the Maas/Waal Canal. They were to seize bridges across these waterways, in order to enable the British Guards

XXX Corps 'Rampant Boar'.

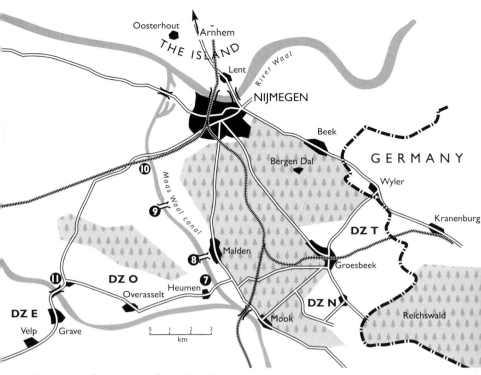

Nijmegen, Grave and Groesbeek area.

Armoured Division, leading XXX Corps, to reach Nijmegen and Arnhem. 505 Parachute Infantry Regiment (PIR) was to drop on DZ November, just south of Groesbeek from where they were to take the Mass Railway Bridge at Molenhoek and secure the south-west portion of the Groesbeek Heights and its LZs. In addition, 2/505 PIR was to assist 504 PIR by attacking the Maas / Waal Canal bridges from the east, thus complying with the Division's experience that a simultaneous attack from both ends of a bridge would succeed. Subsequently, 2/505 would become the divisional reserve. Dropping on DZ Tango, 508 PIR were to secure the high ground between Groesbeek and Nijmegen, overlooking the border with Germany, below and to the east. They were also to send a battalion to the Nijmegen bridges.

The idea of transporting troops into battle by glider was developed alongside military parachuting, as a means of delivering heavy support equipment and stores, as well as non-para-trained infantry, into battle. They were used in small numbers in 1940 during the German capture of Fort Eban Emael and in far greater numbers on D-Day. For MARKET GARDEN, nine hundred CG-4 A Waco gliders were allocated to the 82nd Airborne Division alone. They transported an infantry regiment, three of the Division's four artillery battalions, engineers, medical personnel and other essential equipment, as well as the ubiquitous Jeeps that enabled commanders to move around the divisional area. Most of these gliders were to form a part of the second lift, as the C-47 Skytrains or Dakotas, as the British referred to them, were needed for the parachute drop on Sunday 17 September. So great was the demand on the pool of American glider pilots, that rather than the usual two pilots per Waco, only one was available to fly the cumbersome aircraft. However, unlike the British Glider Pilot Regiment, the American glider pilots were not trained as ground troops but, in this case, as the 82nd was to be cut-off for several days, the US glider pilots worked hard assembling stores. Eventually, when pressure in 505 PIR's sector became dangerous, they held a section of line. Eventually they were returned down Hell's Highway to Brussels, in the process becoming involved in 101st Airborne Division's battles.

During the days leading up to 6 June 1944, General Eisenhower had a very difficult decision to make. Could he launch the D-Day invasion with the weather predicted by Group Captain Stagg or would he have to postpone the vital operation. General Louis Brereton had a similar decision to make based on similar meteorological advice, in mid September: a period of far less stable weather than three months earlier in June. 21st Army Group's post operational report for 16 September 1944 recalls:

'1630 hrs. Lt-Gen BRERETON decided to proceed with Op MARKET. Period 17-20 Sep suitable for airborne ops with fair weather apart from morning fog. Light winds'.

However, what proved to be variable weather conditions over Central and Southeast England and Holland were to have a significant impact on the coming battle, which from its conception had a very slim margin for error.

CHAPTER TWO

THE CAPTURE OF THE BRIDGE AT GRAVE

The tour of 82nd Airborne Division's MARKET GARDEN battlefields starts at the western end of the Grave Bridge that crosses the River Maas, which is located on the **N324** between Nijmegen and Grave (pronounced Gr-ar-ve). On the Bridge's western abutment, heading towards Nijmegen, there is a small area to pull off the road on the crown of the bend. Park without blocking the cycle path. The memorial to the captors of the Bridge is located here and nearby are casemates built by the Dutch in 1936 and used by the Germans in 1944. The sluice building on the Raammond waterway, is often referred to as the 'Power House' by 504 Parachute Infantry Regiment (504 PIR).

The first of 82nd Airborne's aircraft, containing their pathfinders, lifted off from their UK airfields in the Nottingham and Leicester areas at 11.09 hours on Sunday 17 September. By 12.31 hours, the leading elements had landed in Holland and were marking the drop zone, DZ Oscar. Half an hour later the sky between Grave and Nijmegen was throbbing with the roar of aircraft, bearing 7,277 US paratroopers and towing forty-eight Waco and thirty-six British Horsa gliders. Private Joe Watts of Company F, 504 PIR recalls the fly in and drop:

'After a gloomy, drizzly Saturday in England, Sunday, September 17 dawned clear, bright, and sunny, and we were ready. We were briefed with sand-tables and aerial photos taken that morning. Our battalion mission was to secure and hold the bridge crossing the Maas River at Grave, Holland. We would split 2nd Battalion by dropping E Company south of the bridge and the remainder of the battalion, including myself, to drop at the same time but on a DZ on the north side of the river. ... it was a daylight drop which was unusual because our previous two combat jumps had been at night and we didn't know just exactly what that would do for us. We did know we had air superiority, which we hadn't had previously. These things went through our minds but the thing that was worse was the spelling of the objective's name: G-R-A-V-E. That bothered us, but other than that, we thought it was a good plan and we thought that the regiment and the battalion were doing just what they should be

doing to make sure we all survived.

We were issued escape kits, some Dutch Guilders, gas masks and life belts. The word was passed to absolutely not leave your gas mask behind. We trucked to the aircraft, shouting out our aircraft chalk number so the truck would stop and let us off. We didn't stand around long, and the next thing we knew, we were flying over the English Channel and the Schelde Estuary. Somewhere along the way we took off our gas masks and inflatable life belts, kicking some into the Channel and stuffing others under the seat back webbing. Our C-47s were surrounded by US and RAF fighter and bomber aircraft. From a window, I watched a P-51 Mustang go after a motorcyclist riding down a dyke. Just before reaching Grave, the fighter escort seemed to vanish, moving above and to one side of our flights. I recall looking out the aircraft window to see the Maas River Bridge – our objective – and the town coming up on our starboard side as the green light signalled us to jump, from 800 to less than 600 feet. My parachute opened. As I checked my canopy, I could see our C-47s still flying to the north-east, into Germany, as parachutes blossomed behind them all the way to Wyler. Then they banked left on the return to England, and BANG, I hit the ground. I could hear some small-arms fire coming from the vicinity of the bridge. There was flak but not around our DZ. I could see some flak up ahead, blossoming among the C-47s.

As I was unharnessing my parachute, I was busy looking for

C-47 Skytrains heading for enemy-held territory loaded with paratroopers and their equipment.

Krauts, squad members and I watched a couple of C-47s that had been hit by flak as they slowly spun, out of control, to the ground. A couple of parachutes opened from one as the crew bailed out. They looked to be within the lines that we, the 82nd, were forming'.

Captain Moffatt Burriss, commander of Company I, 3/504 PIR, was further down the stream of aircraft, standing in the door of his C-47.

'Below were green, lush flatlands, but we saw a lot of flooding... Moving inland, we saw only miles of aircraft on either side and heard only the steady drone of thousands and thousands of engines. It was a sound that, under different circumstances, would have lulled one to sleep.

Then all hell broke lose. Below, anti-aircraft batteries opened fire, and we saw flaming tracer bullets streaking towards our planes. Immediately, several fighters broke formation and, spitting fire, hurtled towards the guns below. They were quick and effective. Suddenly there were no more tracers, no more white puffs of smoke...

As the jumpmaster of our plane, I continued to stand in the door and observe what was going on around and below us. At one o'clock, I saw the town of Grave and the massive Grave Bridge – one of our objectives. The red light flashed on. I gave the order to stand up and hook up. "This is it", I said to myself.

As we approached the bridge, a 20mm anti-aircraft gun mounted on superstructure of the bridge started firing at us. Tracer streamed towards our plane as we flew directly over the bridge at a height of about 600 feet. Sergeant Johnson, my communications sergeant shook his fist at the German gun crew and shouted, "You dirty Krauts. You just wait a minute and we'll be down there to get you."

General Gavin wrote how, following the Division's experience at Ste-Mère-Église in Normandy:

'Where German anti-aircraft guns were shooting at descending troops, a number of the troopers began firing their pistols at anti-aircraft gunners the moment their parachutes opened and they began to descend. Troopers talking about it later recalled

35

American Colt .45 calibre.

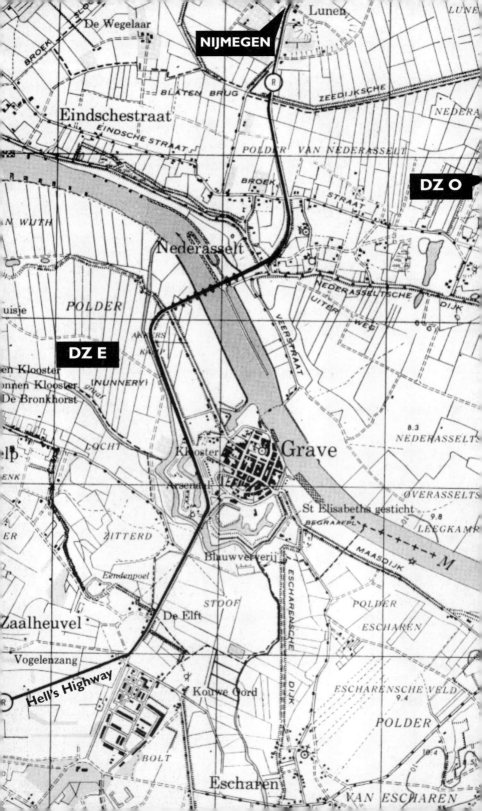

Sluice House

E 504 PIR

Nederasselt

F 504 PIR

Raamond Waterway

MAAS

GRAVE

Guards Armoured Division

A mosaic of airphotographs for briefing 504 Parachute Infantry Regiment

it as being pretty silly because they were just as likely to shoot themselves as the Germans. In retrospect, it also seemed foolish to have engaged a big anti-aircraft gun with .45 caliber pistols, but they did, and most of the Germans broke and ran. ... But we were all pleased with the ability of the troopers to jump in daylight on anti-aircraft positions and destroy them.'

The Grave Bridge – Sunday 17 September 1944

The Grave Bridge over the River Maas, was first of the three largest water obstacles that the Allied Airborne Corps had to seize on XXX Corps's route to Arnhem. The Maas is one of Europe's greatest rivers, second only in significance to the Rhine in its military history. The Maas is known further upstream in France and Belgium as the Meuse. The Grave Bridge was in 1944, the Continent's longest bridge at almost 400 metres in length. The task of securing the bridge was allocated to 504 PIR, nicknamed 'Angels in Baggy Pants'. This Regiment had not taken part in the Normandy campaign due to the lack of battle casualty replacements to make good their losses in Italy over the winter 1943/1944. However, by September, they had behind them both combat experience and up to date training, which were to underpin the 504 PIR's success over the coming weeks.

The main body of 2/504, who were to take the bridge, were to drop on DZ O, a mile to the east of the objective, on the open fields near Overasselt. Private Joe Watts, continues:

'We assembled and moved out south-east along a road dyke to take the north end of the Maas River Bridge. ... We had landed about a mile from the northern end of the approach to the bridge. As we assembled we could see the flak tower by the bridge at this end. It was silent. I can recall, a few farmhouses, occupants out waving at us and calling welcome in English.'

With only light enemy flak positions around the bridge, the airforces were persuaded to drop a company immediately to the west of the bridge (DZ Easy). Thus, two of Brigadier General Gavin's tactical prerequisites for success were met; namely, a drop close to the objective and an attack from both ends of a bridge. Taking the Bridge was considered by General Gavin to be 'essential to the division's survival', as without it, the vital lifeline to the armour of XXX Corps would be lost.

Dropping on DZ E was Captain John Thompson's Company E, 2/504 PRI. Their mission, in the words of General Gavin 'was

The Maas Road Bridge today. The objective of 2nd Battalion, 504 Parachute Infantry Regiment, 82nd Airborne Division.

to seize the western end of the bridge, put up a road block to block any approaches to it, and to takeover the town of Grave'. The Regimental Commander, Colonel Reuben H Tucker has written about his orders and plans:

'Open space or not we always planned to jump right on the target. The Div Comdr – General Gavin – told me he didn't care how I did it, but to get the bridge at Grave. I ordered Company E to jump on the south end of the bridge and the rest of the battalion on the north end. We had no clear DZs but landed on houses, churches, roads, ditches and wherever we came down.'

As the stream of aircraft approached, Lieutenant John Thompson saw the bridge in the distance as he stood in the leading C-47's door, the first man to jump. In no time they were out and descending in full view of their objective, with some fire coming from the outskirts of Grave and from four anti-aircraft positions on the bridge. Lieutenant Thomas, tasked to take the bridge, quickly assembled his platoon on the eastern edge of the DZ and set off towards his objective using the numerous drainage ditches that bisected the area, as cover. The Raammond Waterway was forded with water up to the troopers' necks, forcing them to hold their weapons above their heads. Steadily they worked their way towards the two flak towers at the western end of the bridge. General Gavin describes his men's action:

'The fire was increasing steadily. As they neared the bridge, they noticed German soldiers running from what appeared to be a power plant [a sluice house] *at the southern* [western] *end of the bridge. Assuming that the Germans might have been carrying explosives, they raked the ground between them and the bridge with machine gun fire. Later they found four dead*

39

The Raammond Waterway and Sluice House.

Germans and one wounded. Very soon they noticed that fire from the flack towers was passing over their heads. The flack towers were wooden towers topped by sandbagged walls about shoulder high, from which the occupants were prepared to engage aircraft with 20 mm. anti-aircraft weapons. They were not able to fire at ground troops within a hundred yards or so of the tower.'

At this point, two German trucks roared up the bridge's approach road from the direction of Grave. Bursts of machine gun fire caused the trucks to career off the embankment, spilling soldiers as they went. The uninjured enemy were seen on their way back to Grave by further bursts of machine-gun fire, making good their escape via the same maze of ditches used by Company E. Lieutenant Thompson's troopers, having disposed of the reinforcements, concentrated on the capture of the bridge.

'... a bazooka man worked his way to within twenty feet of the tower and fired three rounds, two going through the gun slits at the top of the tower. The gun ceased firing, and the troopers scrambled up the tower and found two Germans killed and one wounded. They took over the anti-aircraft weapons and at once engaged the German weapons in the flak tower at the other end of the bridge.

At the same time, Thompson had his men break into two teams, working their way around the end of the bridge and across it.'

Meanwhile, Company F and Joe Watts were closing on the other end of the bridge:

'As we closed on the Nederasselt end of the Maas River bridge, it was now a couple of hundred yards to our left front, we began to get incoming small arms fire from just beyond the bridge structure near the river. We didn't get any mortar fire –

40

Pillbox

The Sluice House and Pillbox cleared by Company E, 2/504 PIR.

we could hear mortars some place but they weren't directed at us evidently, but small arms fire kept coming over – we got the "crack" and this stuff passed over us – none of it hit the ground so evidently they were shooting too high. We may not have been the target, I don't know.

About 200 yards down river there was a brick pump house or "waterhouse" as they called it. Every once in a while we could

Shortly after the battle for the Grave Bridge a German anti-aircraft gun in a flak tower, under new management, protects an Allied convoy from possible German air attack.

see Krauts running in and out of the building. ...The track my company was on, junctioned with the main road and to follow it would mean exposure to enemy fire. We left the track and passed through some woods alongside the main road. When we got to about opposite the brick pump house on the river dike, we brought our squads on line along the main road and rushed across in a couple of waves. We were taking sporadic fire from both the pump house and the bridge area. Our goal was to take the bridge approach while suppressing fire from the house and bridge. There were enemy shooters in the bridge structure. We moved without difficulty down the ditch toward the bridge approaches. When we arrived at the north end of the bridge, we assisted clearing the flak tower... We were taking fire from the town [Grave] and initially from the bridge girders high up where at least two German snipers tied themselves to the girders. I kept firing my Thompson sub-machine gun into the girders at them as we made our way to the flak tower by running on the dike shoulders then across the bridge using girders as shelter. A couple of our guys were using entrenching tools on bundles of what looked like communications wire [the German's demolition firing circuits]. As we jogged and dodged across the last of the nine spans, we were running out of places to hide, even though it was getting dark about now, we were still drawing fire from the direction of Grave. Fortunately, a friendly someone was standing at the base of the south flak tower warning us of mines off the dike shoulder to the west, at the base of the flak tower, right where I was headed – someone evidently stationed there to prevent the accident prone of becoming casualties.'

Pillbox

The memorial to the capture of the Grave bridge by E Company 504 PIR. Note the pillbox that was built by the Dutch in 1936 and used by the Germans in 1944.

General Gavin summed up the importance of 2/504's success:

'To us this was the most important bridge of all, since it assured us of linkup with the British XXX Corps.'

The captors of the Grave Bridge painted by military artist James Dietz.

While Companies E and F were consolidating the position and removing wires, detonators and camouflaged charges from the bridge's structure, they were still under fire from the direction of Grave. As an immediate response Captain Thompson and his men retraced their steps back to the bridge ramp and established a roadblock 1,000 metres back along the road to Grave town. With Company E still under fire, Company D also crossed the bridge to attack Grave. As they approached the town, they came under heavy German machine-gun and mortar fire. However, outnumbered by the determined paratroopers, the already shaken Germans were driven from Grave, which was reported as secure at 20.00 hours.

In common with practice elsewhere, the Dutch inhabitants of Grave began a celebration that hampered the preparation of defences, as the population *fêted* their liberators. Tales of singing well into the night are still shared by veterans of the 82nd and

43

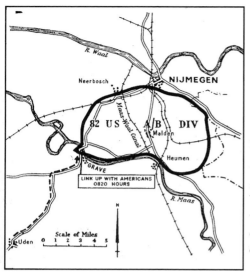

Situation on the morning of 19 September when 2 Household Cavalry Regiment leading XXX Corps, reached 82nd Airborne at Grave.

the Dutch people who still welcome them back for commemorations. However, during the night a tank approached from the direction of Uden and in the darkness and euphoria of success the Americans assumed that it was British. As they approached, the tank opened fire and killed several paratroopers. In a hail of bazooka rounds, the tank withdrew. This was the only occasion when a German counter attack approached anywhere near the Grave Bridge.

During the night of Monday 18 September, the garrison of the Bridge learned that XXX Corps would reach them the following morning. At 08.20 hours on Tuesday 19 September, armoured cars of B Squadron 2/Household Cavalry Regiment (HCR) arrived at the bridge. The HCR's historian describes the meeting:

'The Americans had captured intact this vital steel structure spanning the Maas, a very fine performance indeed, and now the second vital link-up had been effected by the regiment. A brief halt and talk with the commander on the spot elicited the information that Nijmegen bridge, spanning the River Waal, had also been captured. This news unfortunately proved to be quite incorrect.'

At 10.00 hours, the leading Sherman tanks of the Grenadier Guards Group reached the Grave Bridge. However, as 2/HCR's leading troop believed that damage to a bridge further along their designated route to Nijmegen was bad enough to prevent a tank crossing. Therefore, the Grenadiers were diverted, via Overasselt, to a lock bridge at Heumen.

On the morning of Wednesday 20 September, the Welsh Guards held the Grave bridge and the western approaches to Nijmegen. The following day, the leading battalion of 43rd Wessex Division, 4/Dorsets, took over defence of the Bridge.

A mixture of German troops board a Mk V Panther during the late summer of 1944.

The first Sherman tanks of the Grenadier Guards approaching the Grave bridge.

and guarded the vital structure, along with divisional and corps anti-aircraft detachments. These hitherto little used gunners were now an essential element of the defences, as the cumbersome Allied air space control measures and the early autumn weather allowed the *Luftwaffe* to challenge Allied air superiority over the battle area. On 23 September, the Dutch Princess Irene Brigade took over defence of the Grave Bridge.

Royal Netherlands (Princes Irene) Brigade.

Left; Prince Bernhard conversing with Lt. Colonel A.G. de Ruyter van Steveninck, Commander of the Dutch Brigade.

CHAPTER THREE

THE OVERASSELT DZ AND THE MAAS / WAAL CANAL BRIDGES

Follow the **N324** across the Grave bridge towards Nijmegen. After a couple of hundred metres, on reaching the outskirts of **Nederasselt**, take the **right turn**, signposted towards **Overasselt**. You are now following a diversion from the planned route, used by the Grenadier Guards when the Germans blew a bridge on the direct road to Nijmegen. The area to the left between your road and the low wooded ridge, 1,700 metres to the north-east is DZ O. After a mile, on the left of the road, is the memorial to the US 504 Parachute Infantry Regiment.

Drop Zone OSCAR – Sunday 17 September 1944

504 Parachute Infantry Regiment, less Company E, 2/504, used the two distinct parts of DZ O. The two parts of the DZ were well marked by the divisional pathfinders and were easy for pilots to identify, in broad daylight, at the base of the loop created by the Maas and the Maas-Waal Canal. This was the only DZ General Gavin chose to have marked, as 504 PIR had two of the Division's foremost objectives to capture. He preferred to preserve the surprise factor for the other two regiments. The Pathfinders dropped at 12.31 hours and set up

504 PIR, prepare to board C-47 Skytrains. This aircraft type was known to the British as the Dakota.

Dakota W7-Q, on its way to the Netherlands.

their radio beacons and visual markers on the two parts of DZ O. Consequently, the drop was very accurate. The three battalions were able to concentrate and organise themselves quickly and many accounts of this stage of the battle exclaim that 'it was just like an exercise'. There were, however, a few casualties from the inevitable landing accidents. 2/504 PIR's mission to capture the Grave Bridge to the west has been covered. 1/504 PIR's objectives lay to the east along the line of the Maas-Waal Canal, which was spanned by five bridges. In an aid to radio security, designed to defeat German eavesdroppers, the four closest bridges had been nicknumbered, from south to north, 7 – 10 respectively. Colonel Ruben Tucker hoped to secure intact all four of the bridges but the Neerbosch/Honinghuite Canal road and railway bridge (number 10) was a priority, as it was the only crossing known to be able to bear the weight of armour. 3/504 PIR's mission was to secure the main Grave to Nijmegen road, which XXX Corps was planning to use in its drive north. This they achieved with little difficulty. In summary, three battalions were expected to secure over five miles of road and crossings on five miles of canal! A tall order for light troops lacking vehicles, even if they were operating in the enemy's rear-area.

DZ O and the memorial to 504 Parachute Infantry Regiment.

Drive on through Overasselt towards **Heumen**, passing under the motorway bridge. Follow the road through the village of Heumen to the lock on the Mass Waal-Canal and park by the side of the canal. You are standing on the 'island' in the centre of the canal system, where the Germans held out. The memorial, on the building near the bridge, is to the Dutch soldiers who were killed defending the bridge from German attack on 10th May 1940. The wartime bridge was removed in 1990. However, the basic layout of the lock has changed little since its capture by the 82nd. Looking north along the canal, past the modern bridge is the Malden Bridge – Number 8.

The Heumen Bridge – Sunday 17 September 1944

Bridge Number 7 crossed a lock, capable of taking the largest river going barges. This lock bridge was the objective of Captain Thomas B. Heldeson's Company B 1/504 PIR. The German defenders, knowing that they were about to be attacked, by paratroopers who they had seen dropping to the east and west of them, were quickly driven back as the first Americans approached. They withdrew onto the small island between the lock and the broad sluice channel. On the western side of the bridge, engineers and paratroopers of Company B, crawling for-

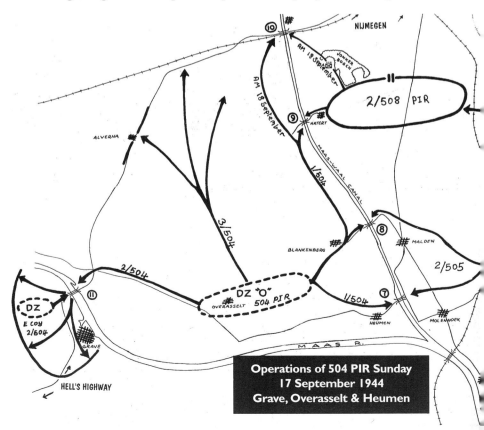

Operations of 504 PIR Sunday 17 September 1944 Grave, Overasselt & Heumen

The central portion of DZ O, which was used by all of 504 PIR less Company E.

Removed at the end of the eighties, the site of the Heumen Lock. The bridge is now a dead end.

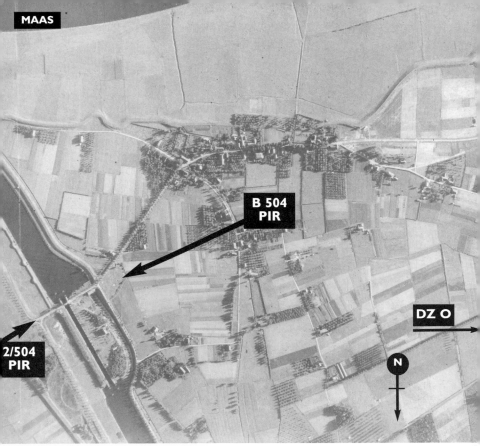

B 504
PIR

DZ O

2/504
PIR

N

Aerial shot of the Heumen Lock taken 10 September 1944.

ward under the cover of their machine-guns cut every cable they could find in an attempt to prevent the Germans blowing the bridge. In the words of their battalion commander,

'They worked with the urgency of men who knew that if they didn't succeed they were likely to go up with the bridge!'

Unable to cross the Sluice Bridge and close with the enemy, Company B's attack ground to a halt on the bank. Bringing up every available machine-gun, the paratroopers poured fire onto the area of the locks, thus preventing the Germans from moving around and possibly, suicidally, attempting to blow the bridge. The German crew of a pre-1942 vintage Russian 75mm anti-tank gun were driven away from their fixed but poorly protected position by the hail of bullets.

The stalemate was eventually broken when paratroopers from 2/505 PIR belatedly arrived. They had been dropped on Kamp near DZ Tango, four miles away just to the north-east of

51

German prisoners in Overasselt, 17 September, 1944.

Groesbeek rather than on the closer DZ November. The Battalion had been deliberately dropped there as there was congestion in the air over DZ N. Consequently they had an extra two miles to march to their objective. Coming down from the Groesbeek heights, they attacked the Germans in what, hitherto, had been their rear. Now surrounded, German resistance crumbled after being subjected to heavy fire and by 18.00 hours

US paratroopers moving through Overasselt.

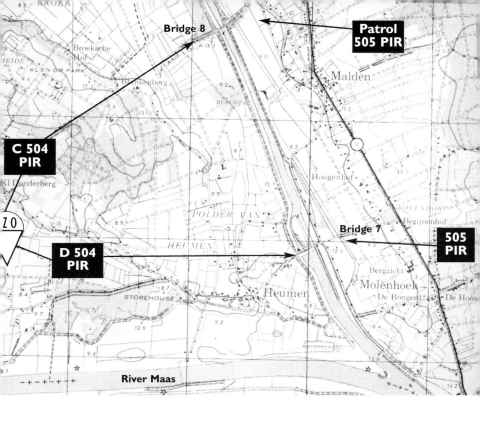

the welcome news of the bridges capture was being received at Brigadier General Gavin's newly established Headquarters.

With the capture of the Heumen Bridge, the 82nd had secured a route for XXX Corps to Nijmegen. However, it was off the direct route and it was not certain that the bridge would carry the weight of armour. The bridges further north along the canal, particularly the large Bridge 10, were urgently required. Bridges 8 and 9 were attacked during the evening of the first day. However, without *coup de main* operations, the German demolition guards were fully alert and had stood their ground despite paratroopers landing to both the east and west. Jumping at the eastern area of DZ O werCompany E C, 1/504 PIR. However, some sticks of paratroopers landed on the low, wooded, glacial moraine ridge that had been formed at the end of the last Ice Age and overlooked the DZ. Company C's objective was Bridge 8 between Malden and Droge. Staff Sergeant Ross S Carter was in one of the sticks that overshot the DZ and found himself dropping towards one of the area's small lakes:

53

US jump casualties and 2/HCR troops at Overasselt.

'I began a desperate manhandling of the chute risers with my aim set on the left bank. Right up to the edge, I thought that I would inevitably fall into that water and drown. But luck had been with me.

A forest of evergreens, the tallest not over fifteen feet, had cushioned my fall and now provided protection. I got the direction of the bridge by observing the planes' line of flight. Then I pushed through the conifers until I came to a trail. A careful scrutiny of my position convinced me that thCompany E would follow the trail towards the bridge. Since I was closest to it, I constituted myself as an advance outpost to guard against ambush and impatiently waited for my buddies. The boys dribbled down the trail in twos and threes until thCompany E was together. Nearly everyone had had a good jump. Within fifteen minutes after falling into Holland we were on the way to the bridge.

Soon we emerged from the comfortable cover of the evergreens and hurried over the mostly open country towards our objective. We were within five hundred yards of it when a tremendous explosion lifted the bridge high into the air and scattered it over a wide area. A few of us got bruised by the flying debris. ... After destroying the bridge, the Germans set up a stout defence in its ruins. We were machine-gunned from several directions. So we lay in the ditch and waited for darkness.

When darkness came thCompany E moved into a wood near the blown-up bridge. We put out sentries, sent out patrols and dug in for the night. Relative quietness settled down over the immediate countryside. Later a patrol from the 505th, which had one hell of a battle judging by the gunfire, contacted us from the other side of the bridge.

54

There was a similar story at Bridge 9. The Germans blew it as the leading platoons of Company A 1/504 PIR approached. Again, coordination for a simultaneous attack on both ends of the bridge, with 3/508 PIR proved to be impossible, as they had been dropped some distance away on the Groesbeek Heights. However, the 82nd Airborne's after-action report records that at 19.40 hours, 1/504 '... seized W (western) side of Bridge 9. Bridge blown'. The same document reports that, having reached their objective after dark, 3/508 PIR sent 'patrols to the site of Bridge 9' on 18 September via the village of Hatert. Presumably, they had been informed by the reliable and well-rehearsed divisional radio net that Bridge 9 was blown and that there was no need to attack it. It is worthy of note the American Paratroopers were able to communicate in the broken and wooded ground. Their British airborne counterparts at Arnhem, however, were only able to establish very local radio nets with their sets, in similar circumstances.

Neerbosch/Honinghuite Bridge (Number 10) – Dawn: Monday 18 September

The area of the Neerbosch / Honinghuite road and rail bridges is now heavily built over and the modern road bridge now carries a dual carriageway **(A326)** into the centre of Nijmegen. The open fields of 1944 have now been covered with houses and industrial buildings as the City of Nijmegen has expanded outwards. A visit to this bridge should be regarded as an option, as the visitor will lose little understanding of the battle if it is missed out. The Neerbosch/Honinghuite Bridge (5 miles to the north of Heumen) can, however, be reached by heading towards Nijmegen on the **A73 autoroute** from the **Huemen Junction** and then onto the **A326**, also towards **Nijmegen**. By taking the **Dukenburg** turning off the first roundabout, going under the Railway Bridge and keeping left, the canal bank and bridge can be found.

The Neerbosch Bridge was the second objective of Company C, 1/504 PIR, attacking from the west and of Company E, 2/508 PIR approaching from the east. On the most direct route for XXX Corps to Nijmegen, Brigadier General Gavin has described the Neerbosch Bridge:

'A railroad bridge crossed the canal beside the highway bridge. Seizure intact was of the uttermost importance to us as

55

**E 504
PIR**

Road
Bridge

10

Rail
Bridge

**C 508
PIR**

MAAS/WAAL CANAL

Nijmegen

The Neerbosch/Honinghuite Bridges.

it was the one bridge between Grave and Nijmegen that I was sure could support the weight of armoured vehicles. The Germans seemed to be aware of this also, for, as we soon learned, they had organized a highly effective defence of entrenchments, pillboxes, and barbed wire. These were in turn, protected by minefields.'

Due to the widely dispersed objectives of 1/504 PIR, the attack on the bridge was to be mounted by platoons who had earlier attacked Bridges 8 and 9. Given the *'uttermost'* importance of seizing this bridge it seems strange that such a small force was allocated to this bridge as a secondary task. The first platoon to approach the bridge was from Company E, 2/508 PIR, commanded by Lieutenant Lloyd Polette, who was one of the bravest and most able junior commanders in the division. Having arrived at Bridge 9 after it had been blown, this company had not become heavily engaged and were consequently able to reach Neerbosch first. Lieutenant Polette made a cautious approach, to Bridge 10 hoping to achieve surprise:

'He moved out at 03.30 hours on the morning of September 18. He was able to move quite close because of the early morning darkness, and later the early-morning sunlight shone into the eyes of the defenders, making it possible for Polette's men to work their way closely up into the German position.'

It was a significant achievement even for such well-trained and experienced paratroopers to get as close to their objective as they managed, with the enemy expecting an attack. However, time and again, the low hours around dawn, when those who watch for the enemy, struggle against tiredness, have been exploited by generations of soldiers. The American paratroopers reached a position within one hundred and fifty yards of the bridge before the defenders opened fire, having been belatedly alerted by their sentries. Lieutenant Polette's platoon was pinned down by the weight of German fire, including mortar rounds fired by a German support section positioned to the east of the canal.

Casualties amongst the attackers, with no fire support, mounted quickly. Fortunately the 82nd's radios were working well and Lieutenant Polette was able to call on Lieutenant Tomlinson and his platoon. Their night attack on Bridge 9, at Hatert, two miles to the south, had ended with the Germans blowing the bridge as they approached. Tomlinson's arrival with his platoon at Bridge 10, however, helped swing the fire fight in the Americans' favour but they lacked the numbers and heavy fire support to press home an attack against the well defended bridge. General Gavin described the final phase of the action:

> 'During the fire-fight they noticed Germans moving about the bridge, whenever they could move, and they attempted to stop them, assuming that they were placing explosives. About 10.30 German demolitions were fired, destroying the Railroad Bridge. Although Polette did not know it at the time, they also seriously damaged the Highway Bridge. About 11.00 AM Polette and Tomlison resumed the attack with 81mm mortar support and overran the German positions. The Germans fled across the bridge to the south-west.'

It seems strange that the Germans only blew the railway bridge. Perhaps this was authorised as a preliminary demolition and they were surprised by the speed and weight of the American attack, or perhaps the charges on the road bridge failed to fire properly. Either way, the paratroopers quickly put the bridge into a state of defence. However, when the Household Cavalry Regiment reached the bridge mid-morning on Tuesday 19 September, their accompanying Royal Engineer 'recce' Sergeant pronounced the bridge unfit for use by armour. A diversion via the smaller but undamaged Heumen Bridge was organised. A few days later, the Neerbosch Bridge crossing was in use after XXX Corps's Royal Engineers had struggled forward through the traffic and over-bridged the damaged structure, thus allowing Club Route to be used as originally planned.

Guards Armoured Division's Deployment – 19 September 1944

Having reached and crossed the Maas at Grave, the leading elements of the Guards Armoured Division were, initially, diverted via the Heumen Bridge, considerably to the south of their planned crossing of the Maas/Waal Canal. The Grenadier Group was tasked to join 2/505 PIR in taking the Nijmegen Bridges. However, tactical air reconnaissance, according to 21st Army Group's report, had identified that the enemy were,

> '... digging-in in the REICHSWALD FOREST area 7852, and it was obvious that the enemy were building up there with a

General Adair Commander of the Guards Division with General
Dempsey.

Late morning 19 September the Guards Armoured Division's
vehicles queue in Overasselt before being called forward to cross
the Heumen Bridge.

view to staging a counter-attack against our RIGHT in the area held by 505 PIR.. ... To meet this threat, COLDSTREAM GUARDS Group from the Guards Armoured Division was put under command of 82nd US Airborne Division.'

Following behind the Grenadiers and Coldstream Groups, were the Welsh Guards who took over defence of the Grave Bridge. While the Irish Guards Group, who had led for much of the way north up 'Hell's Highway', were the divisional reserve.

In summary 504 PIR's drop and operations on the afternoon of 17 September, to take the triangle of country between the River Maas and the Maas/Waal Canal were a success. Speed, surprise and concentration of effort were key elements but where the Germans were given time to regain their balance, they invariably managed to fire their demolitions. However, a route for XXX Corps, via the Heumen Bridge, had been promptly established, without the necessity of time consuming bridging operations by 43 Wessex Division and the RE bridging groups.

Having crossed the Heumen Bridge the Guards Armoured Division with Household Cavalry Regiment Daimler Armoured Cars wait to move forward to do battle in Nijmegen. Note the censor's attempt to obliterate the Heumen town sign and divisional badges on vehicles.

CLUB ROUTE XXX Corps 'Tac' signs marked the route north.

CHAPTER FOUR

MOLENHOEK AND THE HILL

Retrace your steps back into **Heumen**. Turn right and join the **N271** signposted towards **Nijmegen**, **Molenhoek** and **Mook**. Cross the modern high level bridge over the Maas/Waal Canal and at the junction follow the signs towards **Molenhoek** and **Mook**. Take the **N271** south. After a mile and a half, a railway bridge comes into sight. Stop and park in a turning to the left, before going under the bridge. This is the furthest point of the German advance and from here, a path can be followed to the Railway Bridge across the Maas, which was blown on the first day of the battle. The high ground described in this chapter is to the left of the road through Mook and Plasmollen.

Throughout MARKET GARDEN, the narrow strip of land, between the wooded Groesbeek Heights and the River Maas, on which Mook and Molenhoek stand, was an important enemy approach route into the 82nd Airborne's area. 21st Army Group's post operational report describes the intelligence assessment of the area's significance:

> 'It was estimated that as the two villages of MOOK E 7251 and CUYK E 7149 lay at the end of three main reinforcement routes from Germany the enemy would reinforce this area and hold onto these points. This subsequently proved to be correct.'

Despite the disadvantages of being narrow and hemmed in by woods and villages, the capture of the Mook movement corridor offered the Germans the possibility of taking and destroying, the vital Heumen Bridge across the Maas/Waal Canal. *Generalfeldmarschall* Model, always a grand and optimistic planner, identified that a successful attack along this route to Nijmegen, could cut-off and isolate 82nd Airborne. In doing so, he sought to destroy not only 1st Airborne Division isolated at Arnhem but the American paratroopers on the Groesbeek Heights as well.

The Mook and Molenhoek area formed a small part of 505 PIR's front of some five miles that they were to secure on Sunday 17 September. The Regiment's after-action report dated 27 October 1944 describes its overall tasks:

> 'Our mission was to seize and hold the ground stretching from the German border at Reichswald and the area around the

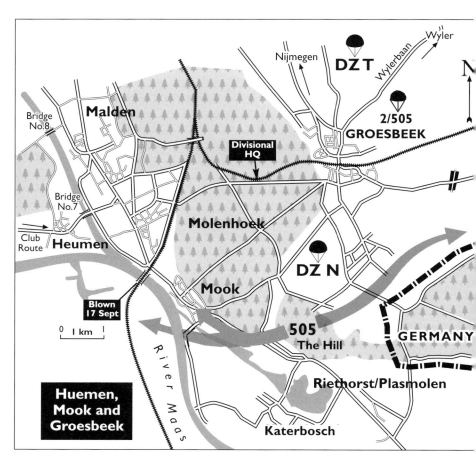

Heumen, Mook and Groesbeek

town of Groesbeek to the Maas River and the Maas-Waal Canal and, also, to aid the 504th in securing the locks at the canal, the railroad bridge just south of it, and the road bridge north of the locks by attacking these points from the east of the Maas Waal Canal. An enemy attack was expected to come from the Reichswald where it was known that the Germans had concentrations of troops and armour. Our regiment was ordered to hold the ground at all costs because on this depended very much the success of the missions of the other two regiments.'

To prevent the enemy moving through the area, roadblocks and outposts were to be established by elements of 1/505 PIR, as the area was too large to be held in detail. The widely dispersed forward companies would have platoons in reserve and further back, a battalion reserve would be dispatched to reinforce the line if the Germans looked like breaking through. 505 PIR's report continues:

'*The First Battalion had already at 13.30 hours, twenty minutes after the jump, about ninety percent of the men assembled. The Commanding Officer, Major Long, ordered the companies to move to their objectives at once. The big threat for the Regiment was the tanks and troops which, according to the report we had received in England should be concentrated in the forest Reichswald. As First Battalion had the area closest to the Reichswald, it was very much concerned as to the correctness of the report. Therefore, at once they questioned civilians about the enemy in the forest. And they were glad to be informed that the report about the 1000 tanks in the Reichswald was false − a statement that was later confirmed over and over again. The First Battalion had the most fighting on the first day in Holland. It was at Riethorst and Mook that the enemy resistance was heaviest.*

The Platoon that defended the roadblock at Riethorst had to withdraw 500 yards and dig in there. The railroad bridge the First Battalion was to seize and defend was demolished when the troops took it.'

The blowing of the Molenhoek Railway Bridge across the River Maas was a potentially serious set back, as its capture intact had been an important element of the MARKET GARDEN plan as an alternative route. The Battalion had jumped onto DZ N, two miles to the north-east but the consequent delay in assembling and reaching the bridge gave the German defenders ample time

The River Mook Railway bridge, blown on 17 September 1944 and rebuilt on the original piers.

to arm the demolition charges. A *coup de main* attack from drop zones immediately adjacent to the bridge could have made a difference. However, in common with the Grave and Nijmegen Bridges, the Germans had prepositioned camouflage explosives at important points in the steel structure of the bridge. All that was needed was to check the electronic firing circuits and insert the various detonators; work that would have taken the German engineers a matter of ten to fifteen minutes to complete. As the American paratroopers approached, the German demolition commander authorised the destruction of the bridge but only as the leading Americans overwhelmed the defences on the northern end. The bridge exploded in the faces of the paratroopers and the centre span of the bridge dropped into the river, making it totally unusable. If the Germans had successfully blown both the Grave Road Bridge and the Molenhoek Rail Bridge, this would have been a disaster for the Allies. In this event a Royal Engineer's bridging column of approximately five hundred vehicles, would have to have been brought up from Bourg Leapold, through forty miles of traffic jams and enemy action on Hell's Highway. The delay would have been considerable before XXX Corps could resume its advance towards Arnhem and the fate of 1st Airborne Division would have been sealed. As already mentioned, at almost every point, the margin of error in the MARKET GARDEN plan was extremely slim.

By late afternoon, a platoon tasked to establish one of the roadblocks was in position on the Molenhoek Road. Their first contacts were with enemy staff-cars, bearing officers racing to the area to either rejoin their commands or simply find out what was happening. One of these was *Oberstleutnant* Harnisch, commander of the *Wherkreise* IV's pioneers, along with a staff officer and driver. Reaching the outskirts of Riethorst at Plasmolen, Harnisch's Opel staff car was ambushed by Lieutenant Weinberg's platoon of US paratroopers of Company B 1/505 PIR. Harnisch died of head wounds while the driver and passenger were taken prisoner. At 20.00 hours on Sunday 17 September, three of 1/505 PIR's platoons were digging-in along the woods on the southern slope of the Groesbeek Heights. Their positions dominated the road to Heumen and Nijmegen. From east to west, they occupied positions as follows, Company B Platoon, Company C Platoon (in the centre) and then

Colonel Ekman and his HQ, 1/505 PIR shortly after ambushing German staff cars near the drop zone.

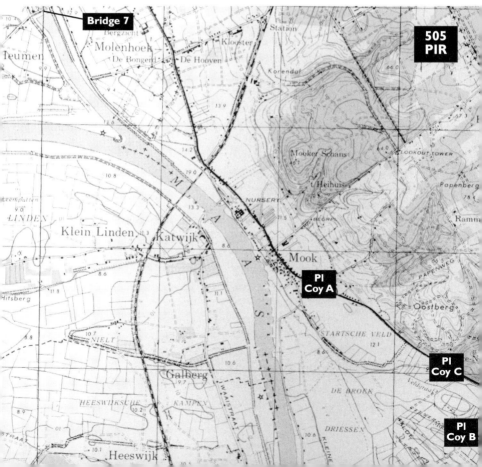

Company A Platoon on the outskirts of Mook. Elements of 2/505 were to the east in the area of Hill 81.8 and the Maas / Waal Canal locks.

The night was, however, not spent quietly. Private Doyle Lawson of Company C recalls:

'Nightfall came and then we heard hobnail boots coming up the road from the south. There must have been a platoon. We scampered to both sides of the road and someone shoved a machine gun at me and we set-up on the east side of the road. Someone else ran to the other side with a submachine-gun.

Ordinarily, we would open fire at close range for surprise and effect, but whoever it was with the submachine-gun yelled "Halt" and everyone opened fire at once. The Germans were scattering in all directions, so I fired low on the ground, right and left. We know that some escaped but most were dead or wounded. When we finally quit fire, no one moved until morning.

When morning came on the 18th, we moved the wounded to the town hall. There were by now too many to handle, so by some agreement, we let the Germans evacuate, with the understanding that all were treated well. The prisoners were sent back to Headquarters.'

Monday 18 September 1944

The author of 505 PIR's report wrote:

'Our first day in Holland had been quiet, but the second day was just the opposite. The real fighting in the campaign started then. ... All our battalions were in action and fighting the enemy. To have any reserve was impossible with a front line over seven miles long to hold. The enemy attacked from all directions, and at some points, we had to withdraw and shorten our lines.

At 07.30 hours, the First Battalion reported that tanks and infantry were moving towards their lines. ... There was activity in all directions. The glider support was to land at 13.00 hours, but as the departure was postponed, it was decided not to clear the LZ of enemy until 12.40 hours. The First Battalion was given the order to clear the LZ, but almost immediately reported that they were being attacked by large numbers of the enemy at Riethorst and that the Germans were moving towards them from the south of Mook.'

Eventually, Company C, 1/505 PIR could be spared and cleared

Private Allen Langdon, Company C, 504 PIR, pictured wounded during June in Normandy.

LZ N only thirty minutes before the gliders touched down at 14.00 hours. Private Allen Langdon recalls:

'The next day we were rushed to the DZ, as the gliders were supposed to come in but the Germans had taken over a part of the landing zone. It was there, just as the gliders were landing, that our CO Capt Anthony Stefanich, was killed in trying to save one of the gliders and its pilot when he landed a little outside of our zone.'

His dying words were: 'We've come a long way together. Tell the boys to do a good job.'

Meanwhile, *ad hoc Kampfgruppen* under *Generalfeldmarschall* Model's overall command, were formed from troops available in situ, along with those from support and training units from the administrative area *Wherkreise*

Captain A Stefanich.

VI. They were quickly grouped under Headquarters 406th Infantry Division and were thrown into battle as they arrived in the Reichswald/Groesbeek area. The results were predictable; for instance, *Kampfgruppe* Gobel's attack on Reithorst, lacking strength, cohesion and fire support, was stopped at close quarters by paratroopers of 1/504 PIR in ambush positions in the villages and along the wood lined roads. In response German armour attempted to manoeuvre in the low lying areas, but found that they suffered the same disadvantages as the tanks of XXX Corps, who were similarly unable to manoeuvre off roads. Consequently, the panzers were easy pray to determined parachute infantrymen, armed with bazookas. These American weapons fired rocket-propelled missiles, with shaped charge warheads that could penetrate the side and armour of all but the heaviest tanks.

Tuesday 19 September was:

'...a quieter day on the front. Only small units of enemy tried now and then to penetrate our lines but were driven back each

time. ... The enemy started to shell our area with artillery: and for the first time, the Luftwaffe started to show that Germany still had an airforce. Both First and Third Battalions were straffed. We had the satisfaction of seeing the British tanks move into our area during the day.

On one of Colonel Ekman's many visits to the frontlines, he had picked up the information that 500 Germans were moving towards Mook and Riethorst from the south [-west]. The Colonel sent this information over the radio to the Regimental CP at once, and the First Battalion prepared to resist the attack.

The 82nd's artillery that had arrived in the previous day's glider lift broke up the German attack. However, evidence was mounting that something was afoot and 'it was with bad feeling that we waited for the new day'.

The Molenhoek Counter-Attack – Wednesday 20 September 1944 (see map page 62)

At this stage in the battle, the Germans clearly understood the importance, to both the 82nd Airborne and XXX Corps, of the bridge over the Heumen lock and they were determined to destroy it. The 505th's report describes the attack:

'About 10.00 hours it started for the First Battalion. About one regiment of Germans attacked at Riethorst and Mook. They were supported by tanks. Our men fought against the tanks with their small arms and bazookas and they fought bravely. The attacking forces were so numerically superior that they couldn't be stopped by the two squads and two 57 mm AT guns south of Mook. Our men killed many and took prisoners in large numbers, but the Nazis continued to advance. At Riethorst two

The Kampfgruppe 'Hermann' advancing on Mook during the early morning of 20 September.

German *Fallschirmjäger* push the Company box and stores in wheelbarrows whilst a *Feldwebel* monitors the progress of the column by bicycle.

platoons, one from Company B and one from Company C, were fighting against one battalion which was supported by three Mk V [Panther] tanks.'

The enemy, *Fallschirmjäger* of *Kampfgruppe* Hermann from II *Fallschirmjäger* Corps, had made their way by train and latterly on foot from the Cologne area. *Generalfeldmarschall* Model had insisted that they were to be immediately committed to reinforce the hard-pressed 406th Division in offensive operations. The *ad hoc* 406th had been fighting increasingly desperate actions against the cream of the Allied armies since shortly after the airborne landings. *Kampfgruppe* Hermann, based on remnants of 5th *Fallschirmjäger* Division, along with anti-aircraft guns and a battery from 6 *Fallschirmjäger* Artillery Regiment, were welcome reinforcements. However, the interrogation of a driver from a German *Fallschirmjäger* unit, captured by the Americans around 10.00 hours, provided information for the following intelligence report:

'PW left KOLON, as did two prcht regts, on Monday morning [18 September]. Regts were to come part of the way by train, then march the rest of the way. PW with a lieutenant was leading a convoy of 30 – 35 vehicles (empty) which PW thought might be used to pick up parachutists at disembarkation from

Germans belonging to the Corps Feldt, take cover in a burnt out farm building.

train. This was merely a surmisal.

Two prcht regt were merely training regts with no [unit identification] number and no combat experience. They had been in FRANCE at the time of the invasion but had been withdrawn to Germany. They have between ten and twenty practice jumps. Strength of each regt is about 2,000 men.

From what the lieutenant said, PW believed his regt was to be located about 3 km SE of REITHORST.'

The German prisoner (PW) also explained that they had crossed the Maas on temporary bridges built by the German engineers south of Midelaar. It is a measure of the Allied loss of air supremacy over the airborne divisions, that targets as easy to engage and destroy as a light military bridge, had been left standing. With adequate fighter-bomber support, Allied ground troops would have not been faced with a series of desperate fights.

H Hour for the German force assembling south and east of Riethorst, with a strength of over a thousand men,

German soldiers running from cover to cover while under fire in the Mook area.

was planned to be at 06.30 hours. However, the attack eventually started at 10.00 hours. *Kampfgruppe* Hermann made steady progress in a north-westerly direction through Riethorst, cutting-off Company C's platoon on The Hill. Private Doyle Lawson was with them:

'A tank had moved up from the east. We were about to be surrounded, so an officer sent word to send someone across the road to stop them. Shelton, Coffin and myself were the ones chosen. I took up position between two houses but the Germans withdrew and laid in a mortar barrage, the likes of which I had not seen before. A shell landed behind me and shrapnel ripped into the calf of my leg, coming up through my map pocket, ripped my coat and helmet and tore the rifle stock into two pieces.

The attack seemed to go on for hours, with the tank pinning everyone down. Our bazooka shells were bouncing off its hull with no effect, so we decided to pool all our explosive into one grenade. Some brave soul crawled close enough to throw it down onto the tank, knocking it out.'

By late morning, the fighting had reached the outskirts of Mook, near the Heumen Bridge. It was the imminent fall of this latter village that brought Major General Gavin hurrying across his divisional area from Nijmegen, the true focus of Allied operations, to face a dangerous threat.

At about 13.30 hours, General Gavin was watching preparations for an Allied attack on the Nijmegen Bridge:

'I had been there about a half-hour when I received a frantic call from Divisional Headquarters. The Chief of Staff told me that both Mook and Beek had been overrun and that the Germans were making their way into our positions there. If I wanted to save both areas from German take over with disastrous

A British carrier knocked out at Plasmolen. German soldiers walk in the direction of Mook along tramrails.

German *Fallschirmjäger* inside an armoured vehicle at Mook using a captured American machine-gun.

A German 20mm Flak self-propelled anti-aircraft gun firing at ground targets near Mook.

consequences, I had to get back and make some decisions about the use of reserves. ... I knew there was a real likelihood of losing Mook and the only bridge over the Mass-Waal Canal at Molenhoek and also losing the Beek and the high ground at Berg-en-Dal.'

The *Fallschirmjäger* were not to know that they had diverted the first key Allied player's attention from the point of main effort – the crossing of the Waal – to a battle that, in strategic terms, was a mere side-show.

With the benefit of superior numbers, *Kampfgruppe* Hermann had pushed 1/505 PIR back out of their forward positions along the 82nd's long south-eastern perimeter. By 14.10 hours, after a deadly game of cat and mouse amongst the town's narrow streets and houses, Mook was almost in German hands.

'At Mook the First Battalion men fought like devils, but the enemy advanced step by step. Mook was being lost. It was the German tanks that broke through our lines. ... At the centre of Mook the two platoons of Company B, now reinforced by the Regimental Reserve, two platoons of Company A, stopped the enemy and a furious hand to hand fighting took place.'

In reality the four platoons, established in stout Dutch houses in Mook, were surrounded and bypassed by the advancing Germans. General Gavin continues his personal account of the battle:

'Driving south out of Molenhoek, in about half a mile we came to a railroad overpass just north of the town of Mook. A two-lane macadamized highway passed under the railroad and into the town. Beyond the underpass to the right was a high dike between fifteen and twenty feet high, erected to hold back the high water of the Mass River. There the dike swung to the south and east, following the river.'

As I arrived, just short of the railroad overpass, a tremendous amount of small-arms fire passed overhead. About twenty-five yards from the railroad overpass a paratrooper was in a foxhole with a bazooka. He seemed a bit shaken, and he was all alone. Just ahead of him mines were laid across the highway under the railroad. Beyond them a British tank [1/Coldstream Guards]

The railway bridge over the Mook - Molenhoek road where the German advance was halted.

Fallschirmjäger lying in wait with an MG-42 – machine gun.

was in position. Just after I arrived the tank apparently decided to withdraw, since the German infantry were coming quite close and the tank was all alone. As it attempted to turn around, a track hit one of the American mines and it was blown from the tank, thus disabling the tank. The crew jumped out and took off to my rear. ... By then, the town was overrun and the Germans were upon us. I had Captain Olson and Sergeant Wood climb up on the railroad bank and engage any German Infantry they could see coming through the town. I then sent the jeep driver back for the Coldstream Guards, with orders for them to double-time to where I was.'

However, the first reinforcements to arrive were from the other battalions of Colonel Ekman's 505th PIR. Shortly afterwards the tanks of Number 3 Squadron 1/Coldstream Guards rolled up. They joined the fighting against *Kampfgruppe* Hermann within 2,000 metres of the Heumen Bridge. However, as German combat power ebbed, after seven hours in action, that of the Allies was building up quickly. During the afternoon the Germans were forced back towards Mook and the Allies,

> *'retook Mook by early evening; and the enemy around the four surrounded platoons of Company B were forced to withdraw.'*

The arrival of the infantry of 5/Coldstream Guards enabled the

Allies to drive the enemy back to Riethorst and under cover of darkness, the Germans withdrew towards the Reichswald.

The outnumbered Americans had acquitted themselves very well but the contrast between the tough experienced US Paratroopers and the young, old and injured German soldiers of *Kampfgruppe* Hermann could not have been greater. The threat to the Heumen Bridge and Club Route was important enough but the attack, in what was effectively the 82nd's rear, had diverted vital attention and resources from the drive to Arnhem. This was to have a profound effect on the outcome of events beyond the Waal at Nijmegen and MARKET GARDEN as a whole.

Subsequent Days

Over the next ten days, the Mook movement corridor continued to be the scene of much fighting, with the focus being on the wooded slopes of the Kikerberg and Hill 77.2 above the village of Riethorst. Following the German attack of 20 September the 82nd were at pains to hold the road with British tanks. After the action on 20 September, the Coldstream Guards Group had returned from Mook to act as the 82nd Airborne's divisional reserve. However, according to 1/Armoured Coldsream Guard's War diary,

'22 Sep. The Regt Group was taken out of command of 82 US Airborne Div and sent south to clear Div Centre Line....'

'Hell's Highway' in 101st Airborne's area had been cut and therefore, instead of armour driving forward to Arnhem, a significant proportion of the force was actually going backwards in order to secure the highly vulnerable MARKET GARDEN line of communication. Their place was taken by the tanks of the Nottinghamshire (Sherwood Rangers) Yeomanry (Notts(SR)Y). This Territorial Army (reserve) regiment was detached from 8 Armoured Brigade and maintained throughout this period at least a squadron of Shermans in the Mook area, in close support to 505 PIR. A brief example of their tasking can be found in their war diary entry for 28 September.

'C Sqn in the early morning were counter-attacked by enemy infantry and tanks. They knocked out four tanks.'

The tanks would deal with enemy attacks along the road or across the open ground. However, the American paratroopers would have to bear the brunt of the fighting, as the enemy

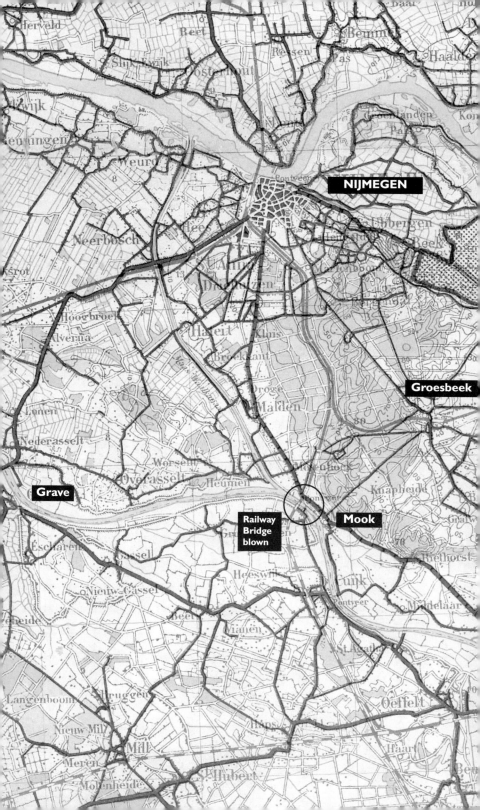

concentrated his efforts in the woods to the north-east of the road. Here, platoons of 1/505 PIR saw some of their most intense fighting of the war. Amidst the trees, they fought a nerve-racking battle at very short range, often cut off and unsure where friend or foe were positioned. The fighting was characterised by German attempts to infiltrate through the woods, interspersed by artillery, mortar and *nebelwerfer* fire. One entry in 505 PIR's operations log records an unlucky direct hit.

'15.40 hrs. Three men dead in one hole along trail at 747506 [above Hotel Plasmolen], *these men may be difficult to identify. They are Sirois, Jewell and Cpl Haag / Coy B.'* Another casualty of the artillery fire was the Old (wind) Mill. A two storey structure built of stone topped with wooden housing that dominated Plasmolen/Riethorst skyline. As an obvious observation point, the Germans were happy to use some of their scarce ammunition in reducing it to rubble. The American artillery forward observation officers held on as long as possible, losing two of their number before abandoning it.

During the fighting, a Dutch civilian sheltered in one of the farmhouses along with sundry domestic animals, including twenty-two rabbits and a mother hen with nine chicks.

'Outside, the Hill was changed into a fortification. Everywhere you looked, you could see foxholes with machine guns and bazookas. As for the Americans, they were perfect gentlemen and gave us plenty of cigarettes and chocolate for the children. They were not best provided for and they were very hungry. We prepared sandwiches for them. They were very grateful and paid me 50 Guilders for the cost. Altogether there were ninety-four men on the Hill with me.'

The defensive positions on the Mook movement corridor were taken over by 325 Glider Infantry Regiment (GIR) shortly after their much delayed arrived in the divisional area on 23 September. The fighting continued with small scale German attacks and attempts to break through the woods and along the Nijmegen road.

Securing the Low Ground 1 – 3 October 1944

The Allies held the line of the Mook to Riethorst road, which, though overlooked, left a triangle of territory between the Maas and the road undefended. This offered the Germans a relatively clear route to the Maas Waal Canal and its bridges and, therefore, had to be eliminated. The Notts(SR)Y war diary for 1 October records the planning of the attack on the villages of Katerbosch and Middelar that controlled enemy access to the area.

'CO attended conference at Div HQ to discuss details of an attack to be put in by the Americans in the south in order to straighten out the line south east of MOOK. B and C Sqns required to take part in this attack. CO visited 325 Combat Team under command of Col Billingslea who is to organize this attack. Sqn and tp ldrs also had a conference with this American colonel.'

The entry for 2 October reads:

'C Sqn and 1 & 3 Bns of 325 Regt took part in an attack from a point 1/2 mile S of Mook. The objective is a line from Riethorst, Katerbosch, Heikaut, Middelaar approximately 1000 yds in all. The attack starts at 0530 without arty sp. Arty concs had been put down last night on known enemy positions but may be repeated on application. B Sqn remained in Mook area in a counter attack role on immediate notice. CO contacted Col Billingslea in his fwd HQ at 0530 hrs. The attack was a success except for a gap in the centre. Col Billingslea put in his third and reserve bn with C Sqn in sp in order to straighten out the line. They were however, unable to clear the enemy out of Heikaut and Middelaar. A night attack was put in to clear Middelaar of enemy. This was only partly successful. The Regt lost two tanks on mines and one badly damaged by HE Fire.'

The attack by 325 PIR and the Notts(SR)Y continued on 3 October. The entry in the Notts(SR)Y war diary written by the Adjutant records that,

'The attack in the south still continues and the Americans tried to clear up posns with 2 Tp of B Sqn in sp.'

The American M1 .30 calibre carbine, widely used by paratroopers.

CHAPTER FIVE

THE GROESBEEK HEIGHTS

During the planning stage of MARKET GARDEN, senior airborne commanders identified the importance of the Groesbeek Heights – a plateau some three hundred feet above the surrounding area that dominated the approaches to Nijmegen. The wooded slopes of the Heights, overlooked XXX Corps' proposed routes from the south-west, as well as German counter-attack routes from the east. General Browning argued, with the support of General Gavin, that, without firmly holding the high ground, seizing the Nijmegen bridges would be pointless, as XXX Corps would be unable to run a gauntlet of fire between Grave and Nijmegen. However, striking the correct balance between securing the Groesbeek Heights and quickly seizing the vital Nijmegen Bridges against the rapidly recovering German forces proved to be an elusive balance.

From Molenhoek continue on under the railway bridge towards **Mook**, which had been secured by 505 PIR on Sunday 17 September. In the centre of town, take the **left turn** signposted to **Groesbeek**. Follow the road uphill into the woods. You will pass on the left the Mook Commonwealth War Graves Commission Cemetery (see Appendix 2 for details). After two miles, **turn right** at the crossroads by the **'tZwaantje Restaurant**. Take the rough **Bisseltsebaan** road through the woods. It is slightly uneven in places but accessible. Watch out for cyclists and pedestrians. After another mile, the visitor arrives at the south-west corner of DZ N. To the north lies the village of Groesbeek and to the north-east is the smaller village of Bredeweg. Beyond this latter village is the German frontier and the dark bulk of the Reichswald.

CWGC Cemetery on the road between Mook and Groesbeek.

A 'Stick' from 3/505 Bn, jump from a Dakota troop carrier.

Drop Zone N (November) – Sunday 17 September 1944

Brigadier General Gavin, standing in the door of his C-47, ready to jump attempted to follow the fly-in on his map:

> *'I did not recognize the terrain when suddenly ahead the Grave bridge came into sight. Some ack-ack was coming up from it. We went on and in seconds, I could see the Groesbeek high*

US 82nd Airborne drop into Groesbeek, 17 September.

ground just ahead of us. Along the woods, as we approached, could be seen a newly dug trench system that extended for quite some distance. Small arms fire was coming up from it. As the ground rose, it seemed to be very close to us, and everything that I had memorized was coming into sight. The triangular patch of woods near where I was to jump appeared under us as the jump light went on. Although we seemed quite close to the ground, we went out without a seconds delay, and we seemed to hit the ground almost at once. Heavily laden with ammunition, weapons, grenades, I had a hard landing while the parachute was still oscillating. At once we were under small-arms fire coming from nearby woods.'

General Gavin had in fact badly injured his back and went on to fight the entire battle in considerable pain and discomfort! Having landed, such opposition as there was fired a few shots and wisely retired as the paratroopers bore down on them. All, however, did not go totally to plan. At one stage, two streams of C-47 aircraft were, converging above the DZ at the same time and were, consequently, in danger of dropping their paratroopers on one another. 2/505 PIR, as already mentioned, was quickly diverted to a secondary DZ north-west of Groesbeek near Kamp. Here despite understandable disorientation, the battalion quickly assembled and marched south through Groesbeek to its intended positions around Hill 81.8.

Following the paratroopers, in a glider that landed on the now secured LZ, was Cyril Wray, of the BBC, one of the two corespondents accredited to 82nd Airborne. He describes his initial impression of the American Paratroopers:

'The 82nd was a good division, extremely professional, but approached the battle like bloodthirsty boy scouts, armed to the

Looking across 2/505 PIR's DZ between Groesbeek and Kamp. The Reichswald is on skyline three miles away.

Job done – an abandoned glider on LZ N is inspected by Dutch civilians.

teeth. Grenades hanging all over them. Our gliders landed in the centre of a circle held by paratroops who had dropped previously. The American soldiers stormed out of the gliders, armed to the teeth, and met two cows and a Dutch farmer. Then they started to dig in, in a peaceful landscape of hills and woods.'

While the DZ and LZ may have been relatively quiet when the gliders arrived, Wray's American colleague, Bill Boni, quickly learnt that the surrounding woods were far from clear of enemy.

'I believe we landed in the Groesbeek area [he did]. The landing I can recall as having been made in what had been a turnip field. Much of it was ploughed soil, and that was the part where our glider landed with relatively little incident. The Lieutenant in charge of a Recon Platoon offered to take us along, since he was going out to look for stray Germans.

It was on a sand road through the woods, north of there and running from the Mook-Nijmegen highway towards Berg en Dal, that we found this little hotel. There we re-encountered the Recon lieutenant, with quite a cluster of POWs. On the day we landed there was actually, very little gunfire we were aware of. Later, we busied ourselves digging foxholes when it became clear that there would be some shelling...'

Brigadier General Gavin, with a commander's sense of urgency, led the way off the DZ:

'My immediate problem was to take my headquarters group

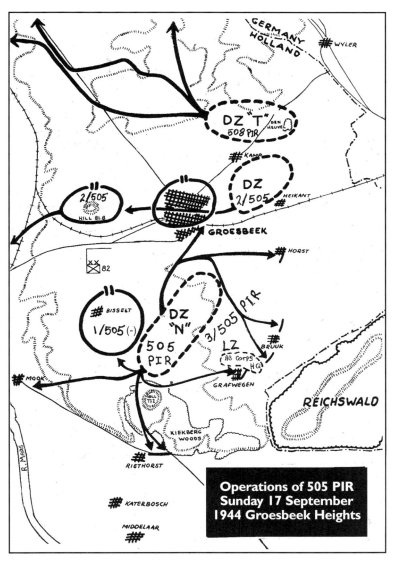

Operations of 505 PIR Sunday 17 September 1944 Groesbeek Heights

to the site we had selected for our divisional command post. It was in the woods about a mile away, but the simplest and surest way to get to it was to follow a dirt road to the outskirts of Groesbeek and then turn back on the paved road that would bring us right to the command post ... The only "infantry" I had with me were engineers, so I told one of the officers to send out a point and start down the dirt road to Groesbeek without delay.

Lt. A.D. Bestebreurtje, 82nd Airborne's Dutch liaison officer.

They were extremely timid because of the firing that had taken place, and it was obvious that we would not get to the command post at that rate for a long time, if ever.

Captain Arie Bestebreurtje [a US Army officer of Dutch origin] *was with me, and I told him that he and I would take point – that was that he was to walk on the left side of the road and that I would follow about five yards behind him on the right side of the road. The engineers would follow us and that we would move as fast as we could go. If the Germans shot at us, we would give them the first shot and take care of the situation.*

With his past battle experience, he was just the man for that role, and we started down the road at a very fast clip. It was a sunken road through a heavy pine forest. The banks on both sides of the roads were seven or eight feet high, just a foot or two above our heads. We had gone only about five or ten minutes when a machine-gun fired from just over my head on the right; apparently they were shooting at Bestebreurtje. A small notch-like drainage ditch had been cut into the shoulder of the road, and they apparently had fired down it. The moment the weapon fired, I scrambled up the bank, pushing my rifle ahead of me to engage the Germans. As I stuck my head over the top, I saw a German darting between the trees and running away. I

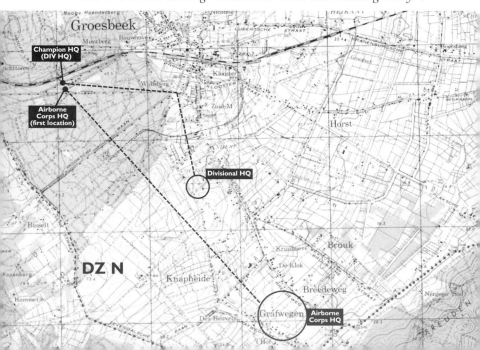

raised my rifle to shoot at him, but I probably would have ricocheted shots off the trees and wounded some of my people if they were in the vicinity. In the meantime, a German machine gun was in position about ten yards ahead of me, pointing at the road. The gunner had been hit in the forehead and was obviously dead, sprawled over the gun. There were no other Germans in sight.'

It is unusual to find a divisional commander advancing with his forward troops, let alone acting as one of a point or scout pair. General Gavin's experience as a combat soldier was coming to the fore.

Also unusual was the 82nd's use of the Dutch telephone system that the British in Arnhem had either not considered or had been too concerned about security to use. Perhaps, the cosmopolitan nature of US society, fed by waves of immigration from Europe, meant that the American paratroopers were less suspicious of foreigners than their British Allies. General Gavin continues:

'In a short time we came to the outskirts [of Groesbeek] *and Bestebreurtje went into a house and got on the telephone. Through a code he was able to communicate to Nijmegen and Arnhem with the Dutch Underground. They told him that the Arnhem landings had taken place and that all seemed to be going well. Without further delay we swung back to the left on the paved road and in another half hour reached the Division*

'Champion' the nickname for the 82nd Airborne Division command post, and the divisional staff at work.

85

Command Post site. I at once went to work with the staff, getting in touch with the parachute regiments and other troops. All seemed to be going well. Later we learned from the Groesbeek police that there had been several thousand Germans in the wooded area outside the town. It had been used as a training area, and it was also the site of an ammunition storage dump. When Nijmegen had been bombed earlier in the day, many of the Germans had fled towards Germany, fearing a ground attack. It was well that they did; otherwise, we would have had to fight even to get to the command post.'

Having jumped at the head of his Division and led the way off the DZ General Gavin was not present to witness the first parachute drop of a complete battalion of artillery. 376 Parachute Field Artillery (376/PFA), including not only its 544 veteran gunners and their twelve 75mm guns but first line scales of seven hundred rounds of ammunition as well. One witness remembers seeing Lieutenant Colonel Wilber Griffith nursing a broken ankle in a wheel barrow: *'I shall never forget the Colonel being trundled from place to place and barking orders for everybody to get assembled at speed.'* Within an hour the regiment was ready for action and prepared to support the rapidly deploying paratroopers. Following behind the field artillery were forty-six of the fifty Waco gliders carrying elements of the 82nd's divisional headquarters, anti-tank battalion and leading sections of other supporting troops including engineers. It is believed that one of the gliders lost from this group

***Generaloberst* Kurt Student.
Fallschirmjäger commander read the Allied orders for MARKET GARDEN.**

crashed south of Vught near the Headquarters of General Kurt Student's newly created *Fallschirmjäger* Army. Whoever this glider belonged to, it was carrying a divisional set of MARKET

Lieutenant General F. A. M. 'Boy' Browning. A rare picture of the General in battledress.

GARDEN plans and these were on the German commander's desk, having being translated, by 18.00 hours. This breach of security enabled *Generaloberst* Student to confirm his suspicions as to the Allies' intent and provided information that allowed the *Luftwaffe* to assemble sufficient aircraft to regain local air superiority as subsequent waves flew in.

Towards the end of the stream of aircraft heading to DZ N were the 38 tugs and the Horsa and Waco gliders of Lieutenant General Browning's Airborne Corps Headquarters. As they crossed the coast they could see the leading waves of C-47 Dakotas returning, on a parallel course, to their base in the UK having dropped their paratroopers. General Browning's glider, piloted by Colonel Chatterton, the senior officer of the Glider Pilot Regiment, narrowly avoided coming to grief on an electricity pylon on the run in to the LZ, loosing a wheel in the process. Their landing was, however, in a relatively soft field of cabbages. The Corps War Diary records at 13.58 hours:

'First Glider of Corps HQ containing Corps Comd landed. Other gliders followed immediately and landed in a good conc. No opposition met on LZ. One mishap on landing – 2 glider pilots injured. 12 enemy surrendered without a fight when the gliders landed.'

Landing near Grafwegen, to the south of the paratroopers,

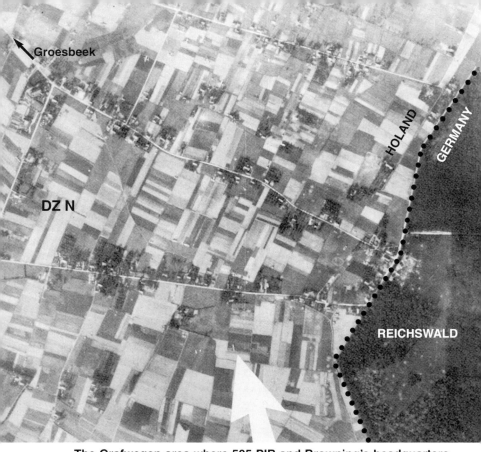

The Grafwegen area where 505 PIR and Browning's headquarters landed. To the right of the photograph is the Reichswald and the German border.

British Horsa gliders of Airborne Corps HQ, which some argue, would have been better employed taking troops to Arnhem on 17 September.

members of Corps Headquarters walked or as some authorities say, *'ran joyfully'* to the edge of the Reichswald crossing the border into Germany in the process. Here, while answering a call of nature, General Browning is reputed to have said *'Ha! I am the first British soldier to piss on Germany'*. This incident was thought to have been apocryphal but at least one Brigadier was a witness and an entry in the Guards Armoured Division's war diary, referring to a patrol that crossed the border some days later said, *'they were the first British unit to enter Germany in this war, apart from Headquarters of the Airborne Corps'.* This diary entry would seem to support the story. Back on the LZ, Colonel Chatterton and his Horsas were being mortared. Those soldiers left to unload the headquarters Jeeps from the gliders promptly took cover. Colonel Chatterton recalls, shortly afterwards that:

'I shall never forget Browning standing above me, looking like some sort of explorer, and asking, "George, whatever in the world are you doing down there?" "I'm bloody well hiding sir." "Well, you can bloody stop hiding. It's time we were going."

Before leaving the LZ, General Browning unwrapped a small package and produced a maroon pennant bearing the sky blue pegasus emblem of British airborne forces. Pennant flying and having relieved themselves in enemy territory, the one hundred and five strong headquarters moved off towards the woods to the north. The next few log entries read:

'1500   Set up first Corps HQ in wood 745533 near CP 82 US AB Div. List of comds and staff handed in. On check, it was found that 27 Horsas and 3 WACO loads out of a total of 32 Horsas and 6 Waco had arrived at RV. One Horsa seen in the Sea. Lt Gee R SIG reported killed by mine leaving DZ.

1800 W/Comdr Brown RAF killed on LZ by strafing ME 109.'

The airborne assault in the Groesbeek area was going well, with Corps HQ mounting an impromptu invasion of Germany. As far as the 82nd Airborne were concerned, they were, as predicted, meeting minimal resistance from low quality and rear echelon troops.

505 PIR's Initial Deployment

As described in the previous chapter, 505 PIR dispatched platoons to hold the Kiekberg Woods and the Hill and to block the road through the Mook movement corridor. Also on the low

Civilians cheer US paratroopers as they arrive in the town of Groesbeek.

ground, platoons from 505 PIR deployed by early evening to assist 504 PIR in the capture of the Huemen and Malden Bridges (see Chapter 3). However, Colonel William Ekman, with a significant portion of his force heading for these objectives, could not hope to defend his area of responsibility in any detail. From the edge of the Kiekberg Woods to Groesbeek he had an arc of three miles of open country to cover with just one battalion. He had no choice but to deploy his men in a light screen of outposts close to the Reichswald and the German frontier backed up by platoons blocking roads and holding other key features. They would identify and attack and hold the enemy until regimental reserves from Bisselt or Groesbeek could counter-attack and blunt the enemy penetration. Supporting 505 PIR were the gunners of 376/PFA, who at 18.00 hours fired their first rounds in support of the platoons that were attempting to establish blocking positions close to the edge of the Reichswald. Despite the artillery fire, the paratroopers had to establish their positions out of effective small arms range of the Reichswald. The vast forest provided plenty of cover to German marksmen, who in good cover, proved to be difficult to suppress with returned fire. The divisional post-operational report summed up 505 PIR's first day in Holland.

'Dropped after the pathfinders at 13.00, seized Groesbeek,

90

occupied its defensive area from Kamp south-east to Mook, cleared its area of enemy and contacted 504 Parachute Infantry at the Maas – Waal Canal bridge at Huemen. All initial missions were accomplished by 20.00 hrs.'

In the woods west of Groesbeek, General Gavin had established his headquarters and during the night of 17 / 18 September he:

'... heard the plaintive wail of a locomotive whistle. I first heard it some distance away, and very quickly, it came near the command post. I had been stretched out on the ground under some pine trees to get some sleep, and I was awakened. ... Having pulled myself to my feet [because of his injured back], I went to the operations centre. I asked a member of the staff to call the 505th in Groesbeek. They told us that the train came right

The South Mill at Groesbeek was used as an observation post by the 82nd

through the town and went on towards Nijmegen. They had not anticipated it and had not attempted to stop it. [It got through to Germany]. When another train tried to run through the divisional area an hour or so later, the locomotive was hit by a bazooka round, which stopped it. Germans came boiling off the train in all directions, and we were rounding them up most of the next day.'

Return to the Mook–Groesbeek road. Turn right and follow the road into **Groesbeek**. On the way into town, by the roundabout stands Groesbeek's South Windmill, which served as a reference point during the initial stages of the battle and subsequently an Observation Post for 505 PIR. From here, they had a good view of most of the approaches to the area. Near to the windmill is a monument that commemorates the evacuation of Groesbeek's civilian population during the period October 1944 to spring 1945, while the town was just behind the front line.

From the Groesbeek South Mill follow the signs to the **Bevrijdingsmuseum** or Liberation Museum through the town centre. The Museum is located on **Wylerbann** on the southern side of the town. See www.crosswinds.net/marketgarden/museumz.html for details of the Museum's opening times etc. The museum stands on the

The Beverijdings Museum at Groesbeek. The dome contains a memorial room, including a list of casualties by division.

edge of the alternative DZ that was used by 2/505 PIR. Well worth a visit.

Turn right out of the museum car park. Continue along **Wylerbaan** towards **Wyler** and onto DZ T. Look out for a metal memorial on your left just before the junction of **Derdebaan** and **Wylerbaan**. This is the dual purpose DZ T and Operation CLIPPER memorial.

The memorial to 508 PIR on Wylerbaan.

Drop Zone T (TANGO) – Sunday 17 September 1944

Prior to leaving RAF Fulbeck, Lieutenant Colonel Mendez, commanding one of Colonel Lindquest's battalions of 508 PIR, fixed the airman responsible for the forty-two C-47 aircraft that were to drop his battalion on DZ T, in the eye. His message to was simple but direct,

'Put us down together in Holland, or put us down in Hell, but put us down together'.

Mendez was no doubt recalling the widely dispersed drop in Normandy and he had no wish to repeat that desperately confused battle he fought on the night of 5/6 June 1944. In daylight, three months later, he had no significant problems with his battalion's drop. Only one aircraft overshot and dropped a stick of paratroopers 2,000 yards beyond the DZ, across the German border.

Shortly after 13.30 hours, 508 PIR started to land on DZ T. In common with experience at DZ N, flak rose to meet the transport aircraft and at least one *Luftwaffe* gun-crew continued to engage the enemy as the paratroopers landed. General Gavin records:

'...a platoon of the 508th deployed and attacked an anti-aircraft battery that was continuing to fire at the air transports.

Defiant POWs from the 82nd Airborne Division, begin their journey to the 'cage'. Despite the general success of the drop, some sticks of paratroopers landed across the border in Germany

It overran the guns and took the Germans prisoners.'
General Gavin continued:

> *'We were all pleased with the ability of the troops to jump in daylight on anti-aircraft positions and destroy them. After Sicily we were told time and again that parachute operations might succeed at night where anti-aircraft could not engage the air transports, but if they ever dared to fly over German anti-aircraft guns in any numbers, they would be totally blown from the skies.'*

The airforce lobby had been proved to be very badly wrong in the 82nd's case and, it is probable that similarly bold actions at the Nijmegen and Arnhem Bridges would have altered the course of MARKET GARDEN.

The drop on the Groesbeek Heights had been as successful as that of 504 PIR on the low ground north of Overasselt. The 505th and 508th dropped 4,511 men in a stream of aircraft that took a full eighteen minutes to cross DZs N and T. In addition, the British and American gliders that followed, brought in seventy

tons of vehicles, equipment and stores. The divisional total for the first lift was 7,467 men but this was only a third of the number dropped or landed by the Allies on the first day of MARKET GARDEN. It is little wonder that as he stood on his study balcony *Generaloberst* Kurt Student observed wistfully:

> '... *wherever I looked I could see aircraft troop transports and aircraft towing gliders ... I was only thinking of my own airborne operations in earlier days. If ever I had such resources at my disposal!*'

508 PIR's Initial Deployment – Sunday 17 September 1944

On the Groesbeek Heights, 508 PIRs's mission was to organize the defence of the north-eastern approaches to the divisional area. The divisional report described their mission.

> *'The Regiment occupied the area immediately east of the Maas Waal Canal and established roadblocks to prevent enemy movement south of a line running east and west through Hatertse.'*

Colonel Lindquest's objectives were as widely spread as 505 PIR's but his principal defensive position was to be established on the high ground overlooking Beek. General Gavin explains that beyond the difficulties of widely dispersed troops, Colonel Lindquist had other problems, a planned *coup de main* on the Nijmegen Bridge having been cancelled:

> *'Next, his mission was a bit **ambiguous**, since he had authorization to take a battalion from Groesbeek – Wyler front, where the glider landings were to take place the next day, if, in his opinion, the situation was quiet enough to permit it. That battalion was then to be committed to the seizure of the Nijmegen bridge. When we looked back on the situation years later, we realized that it should have been obvious that Tucker's 504th was much better prepared to spare a battalion to go to the Nijmegen bridge that night. However, there was no way to determine this on the night of September 17, 1944.'*

Despite these words, there are abiding suspicions that, following the cancellation of the *coup de main*, there had been a misunderstanding between General Gavin, Colonel Lindquest and Lieutenant Colonel Shields Warren. It is thought that this misunderstanding led to the Nijmegen Bridge not being attacked promptly from the DZ, immediately after P Hour. It is alleged that when General Gavin discovered about 18.00 hours

Paratroopers of 508 PIR passing through Groesbeek (Ottenhofstraat) on the evening of 17 September.

that Warren, and 1/508 PIR had not moved on the bridges, he was far from pleased. He promptly ordered Colonel Lindquest *'to delay not a second longer and get the bridge as quickly as possible with Warren's battalion.'*
Thus, 1/508 PIR was instructed to abandon its positions near the Sionshof Hotel, on the main road from Groesbeek to Nijmegen, and advance the three miles to the Waal Bridge. At 20.00 hours, only two companies set out to Nijmegen, as Company C appeared to be disorientated in the woods. The battle for Nijmegen and the bridges is covered in Chapter 7.

Meanwhile, 2/508 PIR moved off the high ground eastwards towards Jonkerbos with little opposition. This battalion launched the attacks on Bridges 9 and 10 on the Maas Waal Canal from the east on the morning of 18 September. However, 3/508 PIR had a closer but more difficult objective to secure in the wooded hills that surrounded the village of Berg en Dal.

In common with the remainder of 82nd Airborne Division, 508 PIR's drop on the Groesbeek Heights had been better than could have been hoped for and opposition was light. Everything was going to plan and maybe the delay in despatching a battalion to secure the Nijmegen Bridge would not matter. However, before midnight, the two companies of

1/508 were fighting a desperate battle with the SS in Nijmegen. Meanwhile on the Groesbeek Heights, the remainder of the Regiment would shortly be fighting for their lives as the Germans closed-in on their isolated positions in the wooded hills north of Groesbeek.

US Army Parachute wings.

First German Counter Attacks – Monday 18 September 1944

From the DZ T memorial, continue down the road towards **Wyler** and stop where the open ground to the east can be clearly seen, with the dark bulk of the Reichswald beyond. Across this open ground the Germans mounted various counter-attacks over the coming days.

Dawn saw the 508 PIR holding a long front that included LZs T and part of N that were due to be used by the Division's second lift later that morning. Shortly after first light, one of Colonel Lindquest's first visitors was his divisional commander:

'At daylight on September 18, when I went to the 508th Command Post, the report was grim. My heart sank. They had failed to get to the [Nijmegen] bridge. The situation of the 1st Battalion was confusing. No one knew what had happened to it. ... and they had left the area almost wide open to the Germans.

I had to get troops back to clear the glider landing zone without delay. I therefore instructed Colonel Lindquest to disengage the 3rd Battalion and move it back to clear the landing zone of Germans. It was a big order, for already Germans were in the woods between Berg-en-Dal and Wyler, and attacking. The 3rd Battalion had been moving and fighting most of the night, and now they had to march six or seven miles back to Wyler, attack and destroy the Germans in the woods, and travel on to clear the landing zone beyond.'

The Germans, who were beginning to cross the frontier in the Wyler area and take up positions in the woods towards Nijmegen, were from 406th Infantry Division. On Sunday 17 September, this 'Division' had been a static headquarters administering a collection training units. The Division's Adjutant, Major Rasch, has described the unexpected

Kranenburg

Reichswald

Wyler

Wylerbaan

Groesbeek

The view to the west across Wylerbaan towards Kranenburg inside Germany.

mobilization:

'Only an expert in such matters can appreciate what it means to change from a barracks-based staff organization, with no equipment or vehicles, and turn it into a mobile field headquarters, all in the space of six hours. ...Our sector, we were told, was to be along the Maas from Venlo to Nijmegen, which we were to occupy with troops that did not yet exist'

On arrival in Holland, 406th Infantry Division was directed to the northern end of their sector, where the 82nd US Airborne Division had already seized a sizeable chunk of their intended area of responsibility. At this point, the German genius in producing *ad hoc* formations came into play. NCO schools, reinforcement and training battalions, as well as battalions made up of soldiers with stomach and ear problems came under command of the 406th Division, along with reluctant *Luftwaffe* units. By dawn on Monday 18 September, a force of approximately four battalions of mixed troops had assembled ready for an attack at 06.30 hours on the American airborne bridgehead. German General Feld, the corps commander responsible for tasking 406th Division, was executing *Generalfeldmarschall* Model's instructions. He has written that:

'It was almost an impossible task for 406th Division to attack picked troops with its motley crowd. But it was necessary to risk the attack in order to forestall an enemy advance to the east, and to deceive him in regard to our strength'.

All together, a force of 2,300 Germans, along with five armoured cars and three half-tracks, mounting quad 20mm flak guns were, by 10.30 hours, advancing towards the most thinly held

98

Quad 20mm flak gun mounted on a halftrack.

sector of the American's perimeter between Groesbeek and Beek. As already covered in the previous chapter, at the same time, on the German left flank, *Kampfgruppe* Gobel attacked Reithorst. Just twenty-four medium mortars supported the whole force but, in common with most German units, the attackers had a high proportion of machine-guns to cover the advancing riflemen. To the German Corps Commander's enduring surprise '... at the beginning, the attack made slow progress everywhere'. However, it soon became apparent that the 'pressed German amateurs' were no match for the tough, battle hardened American paratroopers. One of the battalion commanders, *Hauptman* Gruenenklee, reported over the radio to General Scherbening that his replacement troops were under fire from the flanks and could not move forward. Major Rasch, well forward to the east of Groesbeek with his general, saw the attack begin to falter. As an experienced infantryman he was the natural choice to be sent forward to get the attack going again.

'These old boys lying there, veterans of the First World War, who had just been called up to relieve the younger soldiers manning POW camp battalions. Now they too had been put into the front line. Somebody in the line called out to me, "Major, we've already stormed the Craoneer Heights in 1914!" "Ja," I was able to answer, "Can't you see that its up to us old boys to run the whole show again; and we will do it exactly as we did then. First of all we have to get Tommy on the run, then we've cracked it".'

His stirring words worked and the 'old salts' moved forward again.

As the Germans slowly advanced, General Gavin's concerns grew. 1/508 PIR were, however, on their way back from Nijmegen to clear the glider landing zones that the Germans now held. These LZs were scheduled to be used shortly by 82nd Airborne's second lift. All available troops were summoned to clear the vital ground and, as the planned landing time came and went, the Germans still held the ground. However, Major Rasch recalls how:

'First of all a droning, a buzzing in the ears which developed, rattling and crackling, into a thunderous rumble. Enemy aircraft formations covered the entire sky. Their machine-guns swept the entire area with fire. Bombs exploded in between, it was as though all hell had broken loose. Then gliders came down at every conceivable place. The Americans had predicted our attack and its likely success, and were now throwing new airborne troops into the fight without respite ... gliders were landing as if on a normal field.'

The machine-gunning and bombing of the Germans on the LZs

German 81mm mortar could fire fifteen 3.5 kg bombs out to a range of 2,400 metres inside a minute.

by Allied aircraft finally broke the will of the old, young and infirm enemy infantry. Amidst the landing gliders, they were pursued from the LZ by companies of 505 and 508 PIR pounded by the 75mm guns of 376/PFA. General Feld recalls, in 406th Division's records, that the dramatic appearance of the gliders:

'... caused panic amongst the attackers and that it was only with the greatest difficulty that General Scherbenning and I succeeded in halting our troops in the original jumping off positions.'

The Germans lost at least fifty men killed and one hundred and fifty prisoners. After the attack, the American paratroopers on the Groesbeek Heights were far from at their best and most of them had not slept in the previous thirty-six hours. In that time they had parachuted into Holland, dug a defensive position, marched sixteen miles, fought a sharp battle overnight and marched back to clear the enemy from the LZs. These were exceptional soldiers.

With the LZ secure, the second lift of four hundred and fifty Waco gliders brought in the balance of the divisional troops – most importantly the rest of the divisional artillery. General Gavin now had significant firepower available to him, albeit with limited ammunition. However, he was severely constrained, as he still only had his three parachute infantry regiments with him on the Groesbeek Heights. The division's fourth regiment, 325 GIR, was scheduled to land the following day (19 September) but the 82nd would have to wait a further five days for them to arrive, as they were delayed by successive days of bad weather.

Wyler – The Border Village – Tuesday 19 – Wednesday 20 September 1944

Continue along **Wylerbaan** towards the village of **Wyler**. Park on the Dutch side of the border at the edge of the village.

It had not been fully appreciated that the small and otherwise totally unremarkable village of Wyler straddled the border of Holland and Germany. The 82nd could not initially understand the Germans' violent reaction that any movement into or, indeed, towards Wyler, prompted. The first indication Wyler was a problem was when a company of 3/508 PIR moving to

Waco glider with an airborne 75mm artillery piece aboard.

the north of the DZ towards Wyler came under heavy fire on the afternoon of 17 September. It had been intended to position a road block in the village but over the coming days, it proved to be impossible to hold the village without unacceptable losses to a division that was already thinly spread. The hillside sloping down to Wyler was the scene of many low-level actions where junior commanders and their small groups of men and supporting tanks endured the 'bickering' not dissimilar to that of the 'glory holes' of the Great War. Typical of the action around Wyler are the experiences of Corporal Boccafogli, of Company B

1/508 PIR, whose platoon dug in on the outskirts of the Dutch side of the village. On Tuesday 19 September he recalls that:

> 'I was sent on a patrol into Wyler with Lieutenant Gleim and Private Mendez. We moved cautiously, as we got an eerie feeling as everything was so quiet – not a person to be seen, not even a dog or a cat.
>
> After reporting back to Capt Millsaps that the town was clear, I was ordered to set up a roadblock on the other side of Wyler. We moved to the eastern side of the village and took up positions where the land dropped off towards the swamps on a road that led into some woods where Jerries might hide. We had a 57mm [anti-tank gun] positioned up the hill behind us.
>
> Darkness came on thick and heavy and we strained our eyes into the blackness. The hours passed and nothing happened. Then about dawn I thought I heard the faint sound of a motor coming from the woods. I fixed a grenade launcher on the end of my rifle and loaded a grenade along with the blank cartridge [to propel the grenade] and waited. I knew the grenade would not stop an armoured vehicle, but at least it would alert the 57mm anti-tank gun behind him for action. The engine noise got louder and a truck loaded with German soldiers came into sight and when the truck came within range, I fired the grenade. It fell short, but the 57mm opened up and made a direct hit. Some Jerries were killed but others fled from the truck and escaped.'

This enemy move into Wyler was a part of the general attack on

Looking downhill in a south easterly direction, towards the German border.

Wyler

Groesbeek

DZ T

the 82nd Airborne Division eastern and north-eastern by the three *Kampfgrupen of* General Feldt Corps. The next German attack was better planned. The outnumbered Company B, 508 PIR were under severe pressure and, by the afternoon of Wednesday 20 September they were forced back to the Dutch edge of the village, fighting from house to house. Corporal Boccafogli and his squad withdrew through a barn with the Germans following. They decided to make a stand along the line of a wall, facing the barn.

'Then Private Herbert Ellerbusch did a brave thing. He crawled up behind the wall to an open gate with his bazooka and fired. The rocket set the barn on fire. Ellerbusch had to expose himself in the open to get in position to hit the barn, as a result, Ellerbusch was mortally wounded. Six or seven Jerries came out of the burning barn and surrendered. The other Germans in the barn ran back towards the rear of Wyler.'

Despite making progress, as with 406th Division's attack on the 18th, Corps Feldt ran out of steam against the American paratroopers. However, on the night of 20/21 September, Corporal Boccafogli's Company was permitted to withdraw back up the hill. Being in such close proximity to the enemy, they were receiving both enemy and friendly fire and casualties were mounting. Despite the cover of darkness, the Germans spotted the withdrawal and fired at a haystack and set it on fire with tracer rounds. With the burning haystack illuminating the scene, Company B suffered further casualties during the withdrawal.

The interrogation of prisoners captured between Horst and Wyler during 20 September revealed to the Americans the *ad hoc* nature of the force attacking them.

'Four PWs were from 1st Co, 526 Inf Bn (Str 350 men). Bn made up in KOLON on Sunday and moved from there on Monday [18 September] by train to BEDBURGHAU from which they walked to their present positions West of KRANENBURG. Recd order to attk at 0800 this morning (20th). Two coys in line and one in res. His Bn line of attack was through HORST to GROESBEEK. They were told that to their north a whole flak division was also attacking His personal estimate of the flak division was one company. In PW's Bn were 2 LMGs per coy and no mortars. Our MGs completely broke up their attack. This PW still has an open wound from the Russian

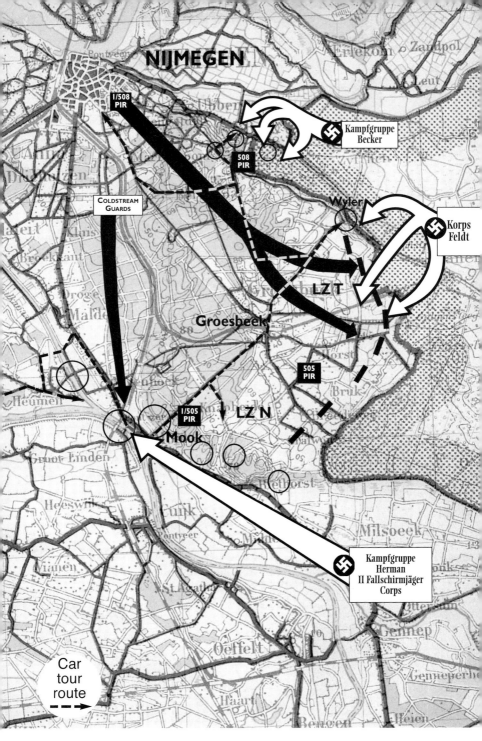

NIJMEGEN

1/508 PIR

Kampfgruppe Becker

508 PIR

COLDSTREAM GUARDS

Wyler

Korps Feldt

LZ T

Groesbeek

505 PIR

1/505 PIR

LZ N

Mook

Groot Linden

Heeswijk

Milsbeek

Kampfgruppe Herman
II Fallschirmjäger Corps

Car tour route

105

The German 7.92mm Model G43 semi-automatic rifle was a limited issue weapon. It was designed to respond to the growing Allied fire power and was found amongst the SS and other special units.

front fighting and was taken from hospital on Sunday to make up this Bn..'

The Horst – Wyler area of the Groesbeek heights, was the scene of much fighting and at least a troop of tanks from the Notts (SR) Yeo were positioned in the area from 22 September, to support the American paratroopers.

Retrace your route back towards **Groesbeek**. To reach the Canadian War Cemetery and memorial wall, turn off **Wylerbaan** onto **Derdebaan**. Follow **Derdebaan** until a crossroads is reached. **Turn right** and the cemetery is on the right three hundred metres further on, in the direction of **Berg en Dal**.

The Groesbeek CWGC Canadian Cemetery and one of the memorial pavillions to the missing.

CHAPTER SIX

BERG EN DAL, BEEK AND DEVIL'S HILL

Turn right out of the Canadian CWGC Cemetery's car park. Follow **Zevenheuvelenweg** in the direction of **Berg en Dal**. As you round the bend on the outskirts of the town, the Liberation Memorial is on the left.

To the north of DZ T lie a range of wooded hills that form a part of the highest point in Holland - all of ninety-five metres above sea level! One of these hills is the Duivelsberg or, as the paratroopers of 508 PIR came to know it, Devil's Hill. Nestling in a valley surrounded by hills is the small town of Berg en Dal,

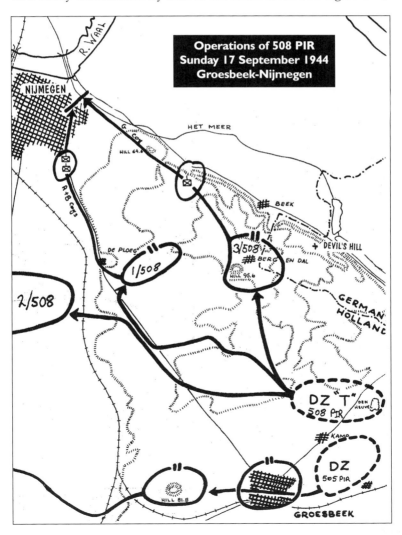

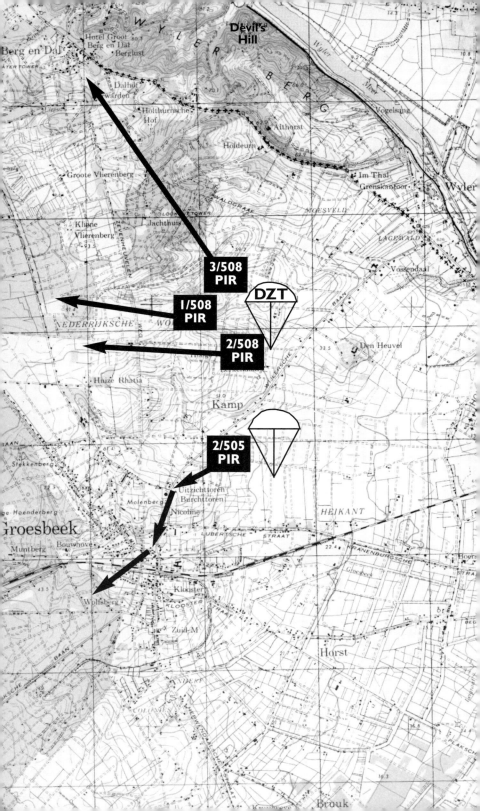

little more than a village in September 1944. Berg en Dal was occupied and held by 3/508 PIR immediately after clearing their DZ on the afternoon of 17 September 1944. Private Henry McLean of Company H was one of the first to reach Berg en Dal:

'Upon assembling, I was told by Lieutenant De Weese to report to Headquarters. I left the group with 12-15 men to go into the town of Berg en Dal. I was told that the bazooka men with me would set up roadblocks on the international highway to Berg en Dal [the road from Wyler].

While the bazooka men were busily setting up their position, I walked over to the Hotel de Groot and went inside. In the dining room, I discovered that the German officers had been ready to sit down and eat their Sunday dinner when they were surprised by the parachute drop. ... Hunger and the sight of food overcame me, so I ate, not one, but two plates full of the delicious dinners.

... Back in the Village Square, I noticed a small café across the street. I decided to investigate the café to see if anything was going on there. Much to my amazement, several people were sitting around talking, apparently oblivious to what was happening. A young girl at the bar asked me, "beer?" Never one to refuse the hand of friendship holding a beer, I accepted. To my surprise, the beer was COLD. To most people that would not be momentous but I had had only warm beer for two years. I will never forget how good that cold beer tasted.'

Private McLean's rendezvous with normality, including a pool table, was cut short by an officer who 'raised hell with me'. McLean rejoined his platoon and assisted in beating off a counter-attack on the Wijlerberg feature to the north-eastern outskirts of the town.

Private McLean continues:

'We bedded down that night in a garden behind the café. At daylight, we were surprised to find a young German soldier sleeping in the Garden with us! While we were interrogating him, a low flying German observation plane flew over us, about 50 feet above our heads. The pilot's face was clearly visible to us. He took us so completely by surprise, we just stared at him and he at us and he flew on by.'

As far as 3/508 PIR were concerned Monday 18 September was relatively quite. The Division's post-action report sums up the day in abbreviated military language:

'Regiment held the high ground vicinity Berg en Dal throughout the 18th against enemy patrols and sporadic enemy artillery action'.

The sporadic artillery fire, however, caused significant casualties. For instance, Lieutenant Garry's platoon despite taking cover in cellars suffered six casualties from German shells bursting in the town. Lieutenant Garry was one of those wounded.

'Long range heavy German artillery landed in front of Hotel de Groot and it took all the meat off Bill Garry's leg from buttocks to the knee. Doc Klein amputated the leg in Nijmegen Hospital. After the operation, Garry seemed to be fine. He was talking and having a cigarette at 11 p.m. He died before morning.'

The Capture of Beek and Devil's Hill – Tuesday 19 September 1944

Thirty six hours after their drop, 3/508 PIR had only secured a tenuous hold on three and a half miles of the Wyler - Nijmegen road, at the foot of the high ground to the north-east. This was another potential counter attack route towards Nijmegen from Germany: Cleve via Kranenburg. Therefore, it was important that 508 PIR established itself in the small town of Beek, a mile downhill from Berg en Dal. 21st Army Group described the opposition facing 508 PIR that had gathered since the afternoon of 17 September.

'In the BEEK area the enemy held the line with about a battalion of infantry, some of whom were dug in and supported by tanks, also dug in, and a number of 88mm guns.'

In the town itself there were probably about a company of infantry. The attack was launched at dawn, with the fire support from the 82nd's divisional artillery, more of which had arrived by glider the previous day. Paratroopers of 3/508 PIR swept into the outskirts of Beek. However, clearing the stout buildings took some time, with the Germans, although outnumbered, putting up stout resistance. By 11.45 hours XXX Corps's Operations watch-keeper was logging a message from Headquarters Guards Armoured Division: 'HCR report enemy beaten off high ground NE of GROESBEEK'. Early in the afternoon, General Gavin passed by during a tour of his divisional area.

'...I moved once again to the 508th sector in which the combat was most intense in the division's area. The pressure continued

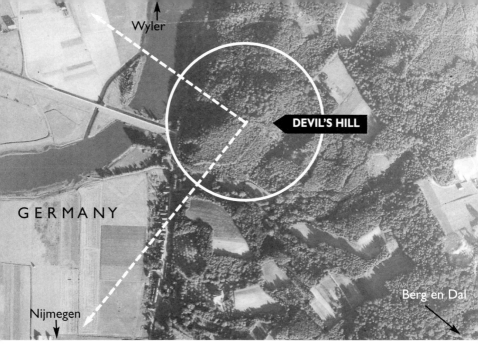

Company A, 508 PIR, captured the wooded high ground that offered good observation and fire positions. The area was defended by German *Fallschirmjäger*.

to mount [in response to the American attack] *all through the wooded area from Beek to Wyler and from Wyler to Groesbeek. I went down through the woods, following the road from Berg-en Dal. The German dead were all about, testifying to the violence of the fighting.'*

Turn right at the T Junction and head towards **Wyler**, passing a large restaurant on the right. After half a mile look out for signs to the **Duivelsberg Restaurant**. The road is single track but there are passing places. Watch out for pedestrians who have *de facto* priority in this whole area. The road is not made up but even the lowest vehicles can reach the bar/restaurant, which is reached by following the road through the woods. Park here. This busy establishment is normally open throughout the day and serves welcome food and drink. The track to the crest of the **Duivelsberg** (the highest point in Holland) is opposite the restaurant. Note the broken ground and trees that led to the desperate and confused close-quarter fighting. It is worth noting that the area was in Germany in 1944. This may partly account for the German determination to hold the feature. A post war border change took the demarcation line to the waterway at the foot of the hill.

As a part of 508 PIR's general advance from Berg en Dal to

the Wyler/Nijmegen road, a platoon from Company G was tasked to secure the wooded high ground of the Duivelsberg. As the highest point on the low ridge of hills, the feature offered good observation and fire positions covering the surrounding countryside. Devil's Hill itself is a ridge about two hundred metres long and no more than thirty metres wide.

As the platoon approached the hill from the west, they came under heavy fire and fell back to their start line. The hill was held by German *Fallschirmjäger* in some strength, with as ever a high proportion of automatic weapons. Not only were the German paratroopers some of the most effective enemy infantry remaining fighting in the West, but the route initially selected by the Americans was up some steep rocky terrain. Reinforced by a squad (approximately ten men) from the platoon manning a nearby roadblock, the Company G platoon repeated the attack but without success. Again they were beaten back by the weight of enemy fire.

With Devil's hill firmly held by the enemy, the mission to secure the feature passed to Lieutenant Foley's Company A, who took the Company G platoon under command. He concluded his orders to his junior commanders with the words 'The hill will be taken at all costs'. The plan this time was to attack from the south. While they were moving around to the new line of departure, guided by a Dutch Resistance volunteer, Germans were spotted approaching from the direction of Wyler. This necessitated dropping off a reinforced squad to block the Germans and from hastily dug shell scrapes, they held the enemy with long-range fire.

In the woods, it was difficult to locate the enemy's main position and during the approach, two scouts and a bazooka pair were killed by a carefully positioned enemy machine-gun on the left flank of

German *Fallschirmjäger* dug in and ready to repel the US airborne assault.

The American .45 calibre Thompson sub machine gun. It was issued to widely in US Airborne Divisions.

the paratroopers. The Company's advance came to a halt. Under cover of rifle fire, an American machine-gun team made its way stealthily through the trees to a fire position that overlooked the enemy position and quickly took them out. Probably alerted by the firing to the south of their main position, a German patrol 'bumped' Company A's left flank but in a brief fire fight it was halted and chased away by a squad of paratroopers. However, in their enthusiasm the squad found that they had managed to penetrate the enemy position and they were effectively cut off from the rest of Company A. Private Angel Romero recalls how:

'The firefight took us up the hill, and we were driven down the other side and cornered in a small ravine. With no place to run for cover and what seemed ten to one in fire power, Sgt Piper asked if we should make a break for it or surrender. Russell Ludemann spoke fluent German and spoke to the Jerries for about two minutes. We were getting complacent when the Germans opened fire. Piper had a Thompson and immediately returned their fire. Someone said, "Lets try to get out, we're done for any way!"

I was at the back and closest to the best exit in the ravine. I ran out towards the top of the hill. I used to run pretty good, and on that day I would have beaten any of today's runners, steroids or no.'

Even though the loss of yet another squad from the main attack was undesirable, it contributed significantly to Company A's success by diverting the enemy's attention from the main approach. The skirmish line advanced up the hill towards the Germans. As they closed in on the enemy, Private John Brickley recalls,

'The sergeant told us to yell like Indians and charge up the hill. We did.' Joe Favela from Regimental Headquarters found himself caught up in the attack by being in the "wrong place at the wrong time".

'When we hit the hill, everyone opened fire. The Germans jumped out of their foxholes and we kept after them. Sergeant Bob White of 3rd Platoon ... attacked on the run over the hill and down the north-east side of the hill. The Germans on that side of the hill had their backs to us. The ones we did not

kill ran down the hill to the woods.'

The German reaction was as usual, positive. Having reached cover, they returned fire and wounded a number of Company A paratroopers. At this stage in an attack, when commanders are moving around reorganizing their soldiers to face a counterattack, they are very vulnerable to enemy fire. One of the platoon commanders was killed and several squad leaders were seriously wounded but having fought through Normandy, soldiers of 508 PIR knew that the Germans would counterattack. On this occasion, the Americans won the race to be organized and managed to beat the *Fallschirmjäger* off before they closed on the new occupants of Devil's Hill. Having been rebuffed by heavy fire, the Germans resorted to stealth under cover of darkness. Private Falvar was sharing a foxhole with the squad BAR man (Browning Automatic Rifle) and stared into the night. The paratroopers were alert but their brains converted every noise and unusual shape into a threat. However, it was not long before the BAR man yelled, 'They are crawling!' and in a burst of wild firing, that was taken up by the rest of the company, he shot a German only ten feet from his foxhole. Nineteen year old Private John Schultz recalls that during the first night on the hill:

'We were on edge with every rustle of the underbrush. We knew we had to conserve our ammunition, but the intermittent fire went on all night as no one was about to take the risk of the enemy using the cover of darkness to regain possession of the high ground.'

The Corps Feldt Attack – Wednesday 20 September 1944

The morning after the capture of Devil's Hill, the defenders, Company A, 1/508 PIR, had only a tenuous contact with their battalion headquarters. Before they could establish proper communications or be re-supplied with food or ammunition, they were again plunged into battle. Major Karl Heinz Becker's *Kampfgruppe,* which consisted of the meagre remnants of 3rd *Fallschirmjäger* Division, reinforced with units from 406th Division, fell on the range of hills that lay just behind Beek. The Headquarters of Corps Fledt, gave Major Becker the task of capturing Beek and the surrounding hills before pushing eastwards to the Maas Waal Canal where he would meet up with Kampfgruppe Herman attacking north via Mook.

114

A survivor of the fighting on Devil's Hill revisits his foxhole.

John Schultz, on Devil's Hill, bleary eyed after a night with little sleep, remembers that:

> 'With morning came noises of motorized equipment at the base of the hill and voices shouting as in preparation for an assault. Then came the mortar fire on our position and we were sure this was the cover for the charge to follow. One shell hit close by and sprayed our foxhole with sand. On my next attempt to fire my rifle, I found it to be jammed. This appeared to be the end for me – I was suddenly useless to help defend our position. I was sure this was it – my one last shot would be my hand grenade, which I stood ready for the exact moment. If I went, at least one kraut was going with me!'

Company A held onto Devil's Hill but the remainder of the Regiment were pushed back from their positions in the woods overlooking the Wyler to Nijmegen Road. For a further four days Company A fought on surrounded by enemy infantry. Albrich Zieggler, who fought briefly with the *Fallschirmjäger Kampfgruppe* Budde, explained that his battalion's mission was to help clear the high ground from the south-east and swing down towards the Maas Waal Canal. Making what he felt would be his last trip to Devil's Hill he told his story with remarkable passion:

'In September 1944, I was only just seventeen years of age. I had been mobilized two months earlier and sent with other boys to a Fallschirmjäger school. I was so proud to be a parachutist and listened to the old salt's stories of 1940 and of Crete but the reality of an infantry fight was different.

After marching all night and waiting in a damp wood all morning, my company passed Wyler on 20 September. The street still had dead and wounded lying as they fell. I had seen dead bodies before from the bombing but it was a shock to see the corpse of a senior veteran that we youngsters looked up to. This frightened us but we were fighting for the borders of the Fatherland.

We went on towards the Duivelsberg. We passed tired dark eyed fellow Fallschirmjäger who would not look us in the eye. This frightened us more and the guides who led us through the wood to our attack point

Fallschirmjäger Oberfeldwebel **captured near Devil's Hill. A veteran of many campaigns, he wears a War Merit Cross 1st Class with swords on his right breast pocket.**

were very cautious. They respected the enemy and we boys looked at each other, fearing the worst. The worst came shortly as we walked through the trees. Brrrrr and the forest was full of bullets. Down went comrades and I hadn't seen anything. I grasped the ground and sheltered in this hollow [which is only a few centimetres deep]. I was terrified and crying. I was only a boy. Eventually I was wounded below my knee and I was picked up by an American and taken in. So ended my first and

116

last battle but as a wounded prisoner on the Duivelsberg, I had to endure our own German shelling for days before I was treated and sent to hospital in Eindhoven.'

Ammunition was running low but the Americans on Devil's Hill had gained an ascendancy in morale over the Germans. Lt Foley was frequently heard exhorting his men to 'Go easy on the ammunition. We are running low.' One morning Sergeant Joe Boon recalls being shouted at as his BAR shattered the pre-dawn silence. 'Who in the hell is wasting ammunition.' Joe Boon replied 'If you think we've wasted ammo, come and take a look!' In front of them lay a row of dead and dying German *fallschirmjäger*.

Four days later, Company A, 508 PIR, were relieved by a company from the 504 PIR. Veterans of both sides look back at the fighting amongst the trees, as their most important engagement of the war. They regard their time on Devil's Hill with a mixture of pride in their achievements, horror at some of the events and regret at the cost.

Return to **Berg en Dal**. Drive through the town taking a right hand turning signposted to **Beek**. Follow the road down the hill and **turn left**. A memorial to the liberation is located near the tuning to the right signed, which is signposted **to Leuth**.

The Corps Feldt's attack of Wednesday 20 September, also fell heavily on the thinly held front at Beek; little more than a mile north of Devil's Hill. Here, only two platoons of American paratroopers held the town.

Supported by 20mm guns and machine-guns mounted in *Hauptman* Freiherr von Fuestenberg's *Hanomag* half-track

Aerial photograph of Beek taken 10 September 1944.

BEEK   Berg en Dal

vehicles, a battalion of Major Becker's *Fallschirmjäger* attacked Beek. The half-tracks poured concentrated fire into buildings, while the infantry hurled stick grenades through windows and charged in. The process of clearing each room in turn was deadly. Attacked, by a superior force but never breaking and running, the two platoons fell back out of Beek and up the hill towards Berg en Dal. However, fighting in Beek became the focus of the action and reinforcements from both sides were sucked into the battle, with attacks, and counter-attacks meeting head-on and dissolving into a bloody close quarter *mêlée*. So focused was the fighting that Brigadier General Gavin wrote:

> *'If the Germans had the wit to move even several hundred yards to the right, they could have walked into the outskirts of Nijmegen almost unmolested.'*

As was the case elsewhere on the front, Corps Feldt's attack lost its momentum. With reinforcements, the superbly trained American paratroopers were able to force the German infantry back down the slope and through the smashed and broken trees towards Beek. By midnight, they were firmly in control of Beek and had again blocked the Wyler - Nijmegen Road. However, in the surrounding woods, the Germans still battled with the thinly spread American defences.

The All American and the Yeoman of England

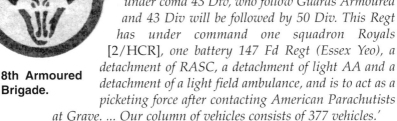

The Nottinghamshire (Sherwood Rangers) Yeomanry (Notts (SR) Yeo), a Territorial Army or reserve unit, were detached from their renowned parent formation. Their War Diary recorded:

> *'8 Armd Bde less this Regiment is to come under comd 43 Div, who follow Guards Armoured and 43 Div will be followed by 50 Div. This Regt has under command one squadron Royals [2/HCR], one battery 147 Fd Regt (Essex Yeo), a detachment of RASC, a detachment of light AA and a detachment of a light field ambulance, and is to act as a picketing force after contacting American Parachutists at Grave. ... Our column of vehicles consists of 377 vehicles.'*

8th Armoured Brigade.

The Regiment, delayed in its move up Hell's Highway by the attack of 107 Panzer Brigade on the newly built Bailey bridge at Son on the evening of 19 September, reached Grave the following day. Here they contacted the 82nd Airborne and came

Trooper of the Reconnaissance Troop Sherwood Rangers Yeomanry, armed with an American carbine, takes cover behind a sentry box on the border between Holland and Germany.

under their command. 'Our role is to support this Division from any form of counter attack,' recorded the Adjutant. The Regiment promptly deployed into action with two squadrons of Sherman tanks and the Recce troop forward, with the third Squadron in reserve. The Regiment's war diary details their locations:

> *'A Squadron with D Sqn ROYALS* [2/HCR] *are to be responsible for the SE sector from WYLER in the north to MOOK south. B Sqn with our own Recce Tp are to be*

British Honey tanks cross into Germany at Ooij with American paratroopers aboard.

responsible for the north from WYLER to NIJMEGEN.'

Recce Troop was equipped with Honey light tanks, mounting 37mm guns, which were mainly for self defence. Their role was to gain information by stealth, without fighting for it. However, to troops such as paratroops, who have few heavy weapons, any tank – even a small one is welcome and pressed into front line service. However, in comparison to the German 88mm, the Honey's gun was tiny. But, nonetheless the paratrooper unused to the luxury of armoured support, initially had grander ideas than just fire support, from the Shermans and Honeys as the Notts (SR) Yeo's regimental history describes:

'The Americans had not as yet had any experience with tanks, and General Gavin asked Colonel Christopherson to "clear the Reichswald"– just like that; as if all we needed to do was to buzz around for a few minutes playing hide and seek among the trees for the German paratroops to come out screaming for mercy. However, we explained the position, and our American allies immediately got the hang of things and co-operated with us in

the most splendid manner.'

Despite the condescending tone of the historian, the two very different military organizations worked extremely well together over the coming days. Corporal John Cropper of B Squadron offers a grass roots view:

'The Americans were a very appreciative lot and were very informal as far as rank etc was concerned, which suited me down to the ground, as we were not the most formal of military units either. ... If we were asked by the infantry to shell a position, we did and worried about getting permission later.'

However, in the words of the regimental historian, the Notts (SR) Yeo found the Americans to be adaptable, *'as well as being most tough and determined fighters'*. The historian goes on to explain how the Yeomanry:

'began to pick up all sorts of American military and other phrases; and in netting-in our wireless sets, the somewhat prim [British] *expression "strength five" was replaced by the more full blooded "booming thru".'*

A letter the Notts(SR)Yeo from General Browning summed up the mutual feelings:

'You have now been working with the 82nd American Airborne Division for a week. You have had a lot of scrappy fighting which inevitably entails very close co-operation with rather small parties – tanks and infantry at troop/company level.

I think I ought to let you know that the American Airborne Division has expressed unstinted praise and admiration for the way in which your people have operated. I am happy to say that when I met your Brigadier yesterday evening, he informed me that you have very much the same opinion of the American Airborne troops.

Men of the Sherwood Rangers and 82nd Airborne paratroopers share a light-hearted moment together.

121

Thank you very much indeed for this very satisfactory exchange of compliments which is entirely due to the co-operation and fighting abilities of your Regiment.'

Nothing pleases an alliance commander more than having his allied units getting on well together.

Returning to the action, on arrival in the Berg en Dal area, first having co-ordinated counter attack plans in and around 1/508's positions, B Squadron was tasked to mount an armed recce. The Recce Troop along with a troop of their larger Sherman brethren cautiously ventured out onto the flat land to the south east of Nijmegen. This area was altogether more suitable for armoured operations than the Reichswald, despite some boggy terrain. The tanks were able to advance,

'as far as Ooij without contacting much opposition and in doing so Captain McKay and his Recce Troop crossed the German frontier and captured a PoW who had been a naval cadet.'

This was the first of several joint Anglo/American operations that eventually saw the front line being pushed forward by 504 PIR to Ubbergen – Ooij on 22 September. The following day an attack by 508 PIR took the frontline towards Beek and Erlecom.

A drive to Ooij is worthwhile, as it takes the visitor out on to the flat low ground that is dominated by the Duivelsberg ridge. The small fields surrounded by drainage ditches, with bridges capable of taking only light weight farm machinery, made cross-country movement by armour extremely difficult.

Sherman M4 with a 75mm gun outside the Groesbeek Museum. This tank has been painted up as one of the Sherwood Rangers Yeomanry vehicles. 'Robin Hood' was the CO's tank.

CHAPTER SEVEN

NIJMEGEN AND THE WAAL BRIDGES

From Ooij and Beek, retrace your steps back through **Berg en Dal**. Leave town following the road to **Heilig Landstichting**. After two miles you will arrive at a roundabout on the main Groesbeek / Nijmegen road. Beyond the metal sculpture, the white building is the **Sionshof Hotel Restaurant**. 1/508 PIR passed this point on the evening of Sunday 17 September 1944 having assembled in the surrounding woods.

Sionshof Hotel located in the centre of the battle area. It was used by journalists covering the battle, officers of the Guards Armoured Division and the 82nd Airborne while in divisional reserve.

The memorial on the wall of the Sionshof Hotel.

The Anglo-American battle in the streets of Nijmegen was one of the most bitterly contested of the MARKET GARDEN campaign. However, with only two reporters accredited to 82nd Airborne, both of whom were busy covering the action on the Groesbeek Heights, there was little contemporary coverage of the ultimately successful Nijmegen battle in either the UK on the US press. Consequently, there has never been the level of interest or knowledge that this highly significant battle deserves. This has led to an enduring underestimation of the achievement of 82nd Airborne Division and Guards Armoured Division in capturing intact the bridges across the Waal and opening of the routes across the Island to the Rhine.

While planning the operation, Lieutenant General 'Boy' Browning considered the problems facing 82nd Airborne in Nijmegen. He believed that the 300-foot high Groesbeek Heights that dominated Nijmegen and its bridges were crucial. Writing after the war, the divisional commander, Brigadier General Gavin, summarized the significance of the high ground on planning the battle.

'The retention and control of the high ground would mean control of the flatlands and the approaches to Nijmegen and the glider landing areas, and would prove to be the key to the success of the over-all Grave–Nijmegen operation.'

Having been denied a *coup de main*, the need to hold the higher ground led to Generals Browning and Gavin relegating the capture of Nijmegen and its bridges to a task,

'that was to be completed after other objectives were secure and sufficient troops could be spared from their defence'.

Explanation of this focus on the force protection rather than the objective, can only be explained in General Gavin's own telling words that:

'Since August the Luftwaffe and the Wehrmacht had been on the defensive and retreating behind the frontier of Germany, so we were inclined to go about our planning with more preoccupation with our own plans than any concerns for the enemy, since his resistance was expected to be negligible.'

In other words, having secured the Groesbeek heights and the glider LZs for subsequent lifts, they expected that there would be ample time and troops to secure the crossings over the Waal.

The city of Nijmegen, lying on the southern bank of the River Waal, was well heeled and neat before battle visited it in 1944.

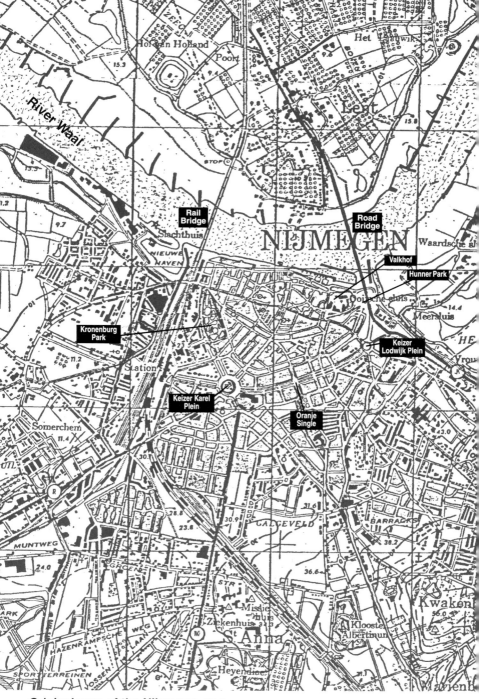

Original map of the Nijmegen area.

Nijmegen had been of strategic importance since Roman times and was guarded by an old fort, the Valkhof that covered the approaches to the crossings. It was only in 1937 that the 600-yard road bridge (including elevated ramps) was built. A second, railway bridge crossed the river from the city's western outskirts, a thousand yards down stream. The old city that lay between the road and rail bridges was a typical maze of streets. However, further from Nijmegen's centre, the newer portions boasted open boulevards and modern features of town planning such as roundabouts (traffic-circles) and dual carriageways such as the Oranje Single.

Sunday 17 September 1944

Follow the **Nijmeegse Sebaan/Groesbeek Weg** into Nijmegen. Turn right onto **Saint Anna Straat** and, in just over a hundred yards, drive on onto the **Keizer Karel Plein** roundabout. Park where you see a space near the roundabout, which can be difficult. Anglo-Saxon drivers should note that while access to the roundabout is controlled by traffic lights, drivers already on the roundabout have to give way to traffic entering from the right.

After a successful jump, the 82nd's three parachute regiments settled down, largely unmolested, to dig-in. Meanwhile, radio operators monitoring the divisional command net eagerly circulated reports of the seizure of the Grave Bridge. As already mentioned there appeared to be some confusion between General Gavin's intentions and Colonel Roy Lindquist's understanding of his mission. At about 18.00 hours, 1/508 PIR abandoned its partly dug trenches and moved to secure the Nijmegen Bridge. At about 22.00 hours Companies A and B 1/508 PIR were briefed and dispatched on their new mission, leaving Company C to follow-on when it managed to find its way to the battalion RV. For the first five miles, Company A had a Dutch Resistance guide who led them to a crossroads in the southern part of the town, where he disappeared never to be seen again. Fed up with waiting, the paratroopers moved forward again. Lieutenant Foley's 1st Platoon of Company A came under fire from a machine-gun a couple of blocks before they reached the Keizer Karel Plein, scattering the point patrol. Private Dikoon returned fire with his BAR, as riflemen crawled into positions to take on the enemy. The firefight was over

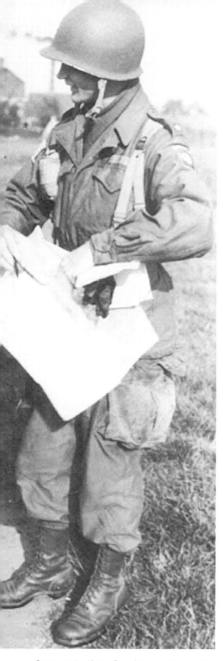

General Jim Gavin realized by early evening that 508 PIR had not moved to take the vital bridge.

quickly and then Lieutenant Colonel Warren, commanding officer 1/508 PIR, encouraged his men forward. 'Good work men! Keep the ball rolling.'

Advancing, the Americans came under fire from the centre of the roundabout and surrounding buildings. In the darkness, Kreizer Karel Plein quickly became the scene of confused fighting. Private Noon recalls how:

'The noise of battle grew quickly, echoing off the surrounding buildings. Lines of tracer criss-crossed the square. I fired blindly as my night vision was eliminated by the flash of grenades and pools of bright light thrown out from burning buildings on the Kraut side of the traffic circle.'

Surprised and engaged by machine guns Company A, 1/508 went to ground. After a sharp fire fight, Lt Folley ordered two bazooka men forward. Within seconds, armour piercing projectiles hit an armoured half-track that had appeared and passed immediately in front of them. Enemy soldiers piled out of the burning vehicle, scattering into the darkness. Corporal Blue was waiting in the shadows at the edge of the square.

'An SS Captain jumped

II SS Panzer Corps commander Willi Bittrich.

SS-*Brigadeführer* Heinz Harmel.

the fence and tried to make his getaway between the houses. I said to Johnson, "Get him with your bayonet." As the captain came between us, Johnson gave a long thrust, completely missed, and his M-1 was dislodged from his hands. ... He reached a tall wooden fence and was trying to scale it and I let him have a short burst of three rounds.'

Enemy reinforcements had arrived in the Keizer Karel Plein.

Earlier on Sunday 17 September, as British parachutes blossomed within sight of his headquarters at Oosterbeek, *Feldmarschall* Model had rapidly appreciated the importance of holding the bridge at Nijmegen if he were to destroy 1st Airborne Division at Arnhem. One of his first acts was to confirm SS-*Gruppenführer* Bittrich's estimate that Nijmegen should be II SS Panzer Corps' *Schwerpunkt* (point of main effort). He also approved the immediate dispatch of 9th *Hoenstaufen* SS Panzer Division's Recce Battalion to Nijmegen, followed by the *Frundsberg Kampfgruppe* (remnants of 10th SS Panzer Division). II SS Panzer Corps' two 'divisions' were in fact each little more than the equivalent strength of a British brigade or US regiment, with a small number of tanks, self-propelled guns and half-tracks. Commanding the *Frundsberg*, SS-*Brigadeführer* Heinz Harmel confirms that:

'My mission was to block the threat in the south long enough to enable the 9 SS to settle with the British Division in Oosterbeek – Arnhem. This was the main task.'

However, shortly after SS-*Hauptsturmführer* Graebner's 9/SS Recce Battalion had crossed the Rhine, 2/Para seized the northern end of the Arnhem Bridge and Nijmegen was effectively isolated from II SS Panzer Corps. Further reinforcement of Nijmegen by the *Frundsberg* was only possible via a flank march and a very slow ferrying operation across the Rhine, at

SS-*Hauptsturmführer* Graebner (left) was immediately despatched by Bittrich (right) to Nijmegen. Within 24 hours of this picture being taken Graebner was dead, but his intervention was vital to the fighting for the Nijmegen Bridge.

On the extreme right is Viktor Graebner of the 9/SS Recce Battalion. Note the *Hohenstaufen* badge.

Pannerden, to the east of Arnhem, or a long march via Emmerich.

Just as the Americans had moved forward to the Kreizer Karel Plein, the sound of gunfire was joined by the roaring engines of armoured half-track vehicles and trucks, the crash of vehicle tailgates and the clatter of metal shod boots on cobble stones. This was the leading elements SS-*Gruppenführer* Bittrich's reinforcements arriving to occupy a key

Rail Bridge

Road Bridge

RIVER WAAL

Valkhof

Hunner Park

Kronenburg Park

Keizer Lodwijk Plein

Station

Keizer Karel Plein

Oranje Single

position – not a moment to soon. The reinforcements joined Nijmegen's *in situ* garrison which consisted of a weak company strength NCO training school, some three infantry companies of

US Paratroopers who entered the town, had difficulty getting citizens to realise a battle was about to be fought in Nijmegen.

Landesschutzen from 6/*Erzatz* Battalion, 406th Division, railway guard and police reserve companies. The first additions were a company of infantry from the Herman Goering Training Regiment which happened to be passing through Nijmegen on the afternoon of 17 September 1944. Another three companies of trainees, from *Ersatz* Battalion 6, were dispatched to Nijmegen, on Model's instructions, from *Wehrkreis* VI. By late evening there were 1,000 men in Nijmegen under the Headquarters of *Fallschirmjäger* Reserve Training Regiment Henke, who also had both 88mm (4th Company, 572 Heavy Flak Battalion) and 20mm anti-aircraft guns under command for use during the ground battle. With his limited force, Colonel Henke formed close defensive positions around the southern end of both railway and road bridges, with his headquarters in the Hof van Holland fort on the northern bank. In addition, Colonel Henke planned to establish strong points at the Keizer Karel Plein and roundabout, half a mile from the bridges, where the routes into Nijmegen focused. Patrols and outposts would complete the screen that protected his main positions around the bridges.

Corporal Blue still on the roundabout recalls:

'We were standing by a large foxhole dug by the Germans when we heard the cocking action of a German machine-gun. McMillan dived for the foxhole and I followed close behind. I looked up and saw Johnson falling towards the hole with tracer bullets striking him. Within two hours, two of my basic training comrades had been killed.

The Germans spotted us and started throwing grenades at our hole. I pushed Johnson's body aside and reached for a phosphorous grenade, pulled the pin and threw it at the machine-gun position. The grenade lit up the area. Blinded by the flash and smoke, I could hear the Germans breaking down their MG and withdrawing.'

The arrival of Company B, 1/508 PIR, and Battalion Headquarters stabilized the situation for the Americans. In the darkness the paratroopers displayed the qualities that had earned them the nickname of 'Red Devils' from the Germans. Private George Lamm recalled:

'Capt Adams ordered 2nd Platoon to pass through 1st and 3rd Platoons, to clear and occupy an area adjacent to Company B about the centre of the circle. This move was a ticklish business. Friendly and enemy soldiers were mixed and there was

131

German trenches

20mm AA gun

1/508 PIR

9th SS Rece Bn

Oranje Single

Keizer Karel Plein today.

no definite line. The darkness contributed to the confusion but also assisted us reorganizing. Instructions were passed to units: "Only fire on orders or eye ball to eye ball defence! Use trench knife or bayonet when possible."

Private Le Boeuf slipped into a Kraut foxhole, still occupied and used his trench knife on the unlucky German. Sergeant Henderson's men checked out foxholes we passed over and collected a couple of AA gun crews [from the gun mounted in the centre of the square], *who were rather on the elderly side.'*

Despite being able to dominate the centre of Keizer Karel Plein, 1/508 could make no further progress towards the bridge that night. The arrival of the SS reinforcements at a crucial point was a defining moment in the battle.

For those wishing to find and visit the **Post Office** described in the following paragraphs, take the **Oranje Single** (the wide road to Arnhem on the eastern side of Keizer Karel Plein). In two hundred metres, turn left onto **V. Sch Straat**. It is suggested that this short excursion be made on foot as the narrow streets and one-way system of the old town can be confusing and finding another parking space a matter of luck.

One piece of information that the local resistance immediately passed to General Gavin's Headquarters was that the Nijmegen Post Office, about 500 yards from the bridges, was where one of the firing mechanisms for the demolition charges was located. Obviously, its capture and destruction was an important priority if 508 PIR were to stand a chance of capturing the bridges intact. While the battle was raging at the Keizer Karel Plein, a patrol from 1/508 PIR slipped through the German outposts and attacked the Post Office building. After a short but sharp firefight the building was secured and what was supposed to be the firing mechanism was destroyed. As ever, the Germans responded quickly and the paratroopers were surrounded in the building, where they fought for three days, while their ammunition, food and water dwindled and their casualties mounted.

The belated American probe into Nijmegen had failed to take the bridges and without a coherent plan to overcome the unexpectedly strong German defences, 1/508 withdrew to reorganize. They were regrouping on the southern outskirts of the city when General Gavin's order came for them to make a forced march back to Groesbeek, where the situation had deteriorated, with Corps Feldt occupying the vital landing zones. Back in the city, the Germans set about developing positions as further elements of *Kampfgruppe Frundsberg* arrived, with SS-*Hauptsturmführer* Euling taking over responsibility for the close defence of the road bridge.

Monday 18 September 1944

While most of 1/508 PIR were counter-marching back to the Groesbeek heights, Company G, 3/508 remained in the city. In the face of the crisis caused by German 406th Division's attack on the LZs, a company was all that could be spared for another attempt to take the 82nd's principal objective.

As the previous evening's attempt to seize the road bridge had been halted by the Keizer Karel Plein strongpoint, Company G, therefore, took an easterly route towards their objective around the outskirts of the town. However, by the following morning, the German screen and strong points had been reinforced by further SS troops but the majority were mainly, as originally expected, rear echelon troops. The battle hardened paratroopers, with the benefit of daylight and knowing that there was a significant force of Germans defending the bridges, made determined progress. Carefully avoiding the major strong points, they brushed aside the

German outposts, as they quickly but methodically cleared the buildings along their route. At this point the German artillery intervened when the remnants of SS-*Hauptsturmführer* Schwappacher's SS Artillery Training Replacement Regiment V, in position just north of the river, engaged the Americans who were approaching the road bridge's main defences. His after action report records how the Police Reservists, who were acting as infantry,

'... were already streaming back to the rear, when the attack was brought to a halt with precise salvos dropped amongst the leading waves. Our own [SS] infantry now reinforced from the rear and supported by further artillery fire, were able to force the enemy well back to the south. The northern roundabouts came back into our possession.'

The presence of the experienced and aggressive SS panzer grenadiers, supported by significant artillery, swung the balance in favour of the Germans. However, Company G, 3/508 PIR, had very nearly succeeded in reaching the bridge. For a single company to have reached a point within a hundred yards of their objective was a tremendous achievement.

SS-*Sturmbannführer* Leo Reinhold defender of Nijmegen.

During the ensuing lull in the battle for Nijmegen, the SS soldiers of the rapidly forming *Kampfgruppe* Reinhold took over the co-ordination and development of the defensive positions. SS-*Sturmbannführer* Reinhold set up his command post on the northern bank, with *Fallschirmjäger* Colonel Henke responsible for the rail bridge and SS-*Hauptsturmführer* Euling consolidating positions around the road bridge. Tactics remained unchanged; there was an outpost line based on the dual carriageway and two roundabouts, with strong points established at key junctions. The main positions were kept tight around the two bridges and progressively strengthened over the next forty-eight hours, as SS infantry, armour and artillery units from the *Frundsberg* were ferried across the Rhine at Pannerden on to the Island. The Germans' growing strength in both quantity and quality meant that *Generalfeldmarschall* Model could stand by his insistence that the Nijmegen bridges should not be blown with some justification. Such was the strength of the German positions in Nijmegen, the Allies would have to await the arrival of XXX Corps' armour if they were to have any chance of taking the bridge. With the delay in breaking-out of the Neerpeldt Bridgehead and the blowing of the Son Bridge MARKET GARDEN was already well behind schedule.

Tuesday 19 September 1944

Shortly after the arrival of the Grenadier Group at Grave, the airborne commander, General Browning, met General Horrocks of XXX Corps, accompanied by Major General Adair, in Molenhoek, for the first time. The result was orders for the Grenadiers to mount an attack, with the Americans, on the Nijmegen bridges. General Gavin recorded the decisions:

*'Despite the thinness of our infantry on the Groesbeek –
Wyler front, I now felt that I could spare the divisional reserve,
Ben Vandervoort's 2nd Battalion of the 505th. I discussed this
with General Browning and an officer from the Guards
Armoured Division. Vandervoort was attached to the Grenadier
Guards and was at once committed to the battle for the southern
end of the Nijmegen Bridge. To replace Vandervoort in divisional
reserve, a battalion of the Coldstream Guards was attached to the
82nd. I directed that they be moved to the general vicinity of
where Vandervoort had been* [Sionshof]. *It was most reassuring*

A scout car belonging to 5/Coldstream Guards with its commander being briefed on the situation in Nijmegen 19 September.

to have the linkup [with XXX Corps] *occur. Not only did it permit me to commit Vandervoort to the capture of the southern end of the Nijmegen Bridge; it now freed the 504th for further use.*

Diamler armoured car belonging to the 2nd Household Cavalry Regiment.

The Daimler armoured cars of 2/HCR led the Guards Armoured Division into Nijmegen and deployed in an arc to observe the river and the city's eastern and western flanks. Usually seeking to avoid engagements with the enemy, the Household Cavalrymen were in the unusual situation of their 2-pounder guns being the heaviest weapon available. The Americans pressed them to engage enemy positions that were making life difficult for them. In one such incident, the Germans, in the form of two dug-in 88mm guns, had been firing across the river from the area of Lent. Firing at maximum range the HCR's 2-pounder guns drove the Germans gunners from their guns. However, pleasure at the enemy's discomfort was short lived, when a further, hitherto silent, 88mm opened fire but this gun was well camouflaged and out of the diminutive 2-pounder's range. Meanwhile, the Guards divisional artillery was reporting 'ready for action'. The 88mm's grid reference was passed accurately and the first salvo from six 25-pounders found its target. For a while the battle escalated, as the enemy responded by bringing SS-*Hauptsturmführer* Schwappacher's artillery into action. Soon 105mm rounds were bursting around the Allies. Captain Cooper left his Daimler and joined the paratroopers on the ground:

'I decided to get into a trench with the Americans and stayed there for one and a half hours, by which time I was completely deaf and covered with dust. "This sort of shelling is perfectly bloody and gives you a splitting headache and seems to jar the whole system. Every now and again, the spandaus opened up from the other side of the river and bullets whistled over our heads. These American troops are splendid types – extremely brave, cheerful and indifferent to the worst. The bridge, an enormous girdered affair, has been wired for blowing, which the

"underground" have twice cut, and is covered by every conceivable German weapon.'

While 2/HCR were doing their bit to even up the firefight on the riverbank, the Grenadier Group and 2/504 PIR were preparing a concerted attack on the well dug-in and reinforced Germans at the two bridges. The Post Office was a subsidiary task for the group attacking the road bridge, as nothing had been heard from the paratroopers who had stormed it on Sunday night. The force was split into two columns:

Western Force	Eastern Force
Objective: Railway Bridge	**Objective:** Road Bridge
1 troop of tanks from No.3 Squadron, 2/Grenadiers.	3 troops of tanks from No.3 Squadron, 2/Grenadiers.
1 platoon of infantry from No. 2 Company, 1/Grenadiers (mounted in carriers).	3 Platoons of infantry from No.2 Company, 1/Grenadiers.
Company D, 2/505 PIR.	Companies E and F, 2/505 PIR.

A German 105mm artillery piece in action near Nijmegen.

Lieutenant Dawson in this area

Oranje Single

Keizer Lodwijk Plein

To Bridge

Hunner Park

Valkhof

Keizer Lodwijk Plein is today still over looked by the houses from which Lieutenant Dawson engaged the Germans dug-in in the area to his front.

The main through carriageway of **Oranje Single** has a local traffic road running parallel. Turn onto the local traffic road. After crossing **Berg en Dalseweg** look for a parking place and walk on towards the southern side of **Keizer Traianus Plein** (formerly Keizer Lodwijk Plein), where the area of the fighting of 19 September can be viewed.

The plan was for the two forces to seize the bridges, by making an armoured dash through the streets of Nijmegen, led by Dutch guides riding in the leading tanks' turrets. H Hour was 16.00 hours and both forces set off at speed, with American paratroopers riding on the back of the tanks. Lieutenant Moller's Sherman, leading the Eastern Force came under fire as it entered the open Keizer Lodwijk Plein, about 300 metres from the bridge. Since Sunday's encounter battle, the Germans had enhanced the fortifications at the southern end of the road bridge, making excellent use of the surrounding houses and the Valkhof, an old fort that dominated the area. In addition, they had dug deep trenches and had even converted the bandstand into a strongpoint with good fields of fire. In the opening exchange, the leading British tank and a German anti-tank gun were knocked-out. Two further tanks were knocked out by a pair of 88mm guns near the bridge. The paratroopers had at first contact with the enemy, leapt off the tanks and fanned out into the surrounding buildings. It proved impossible for them to advance through the machine-gun fire that swept the square in front of the German anti-tank guns. The Grenadiers' Number 2 Company were following at the rear of the column and attempted to outflank the German positions but also ran in to a wall of fire as they emerged from the side streets. The Guard's divisional historian recalls that a temporary advantage was secured when:

'Lieutenant Dawson found a view-point in a house from which he could overlook the German positions and, after bringing up all available automatic weapons, opened up on the enemy in front. A considerable number were killed and wounded but fire was returned by an 88mm gun; this scored a direct hit on the house which had to be evacuated.'

As darkness set in, it was now all to obvious too the Allies that the enemy was strongly holding the approaches to the bridge and that despite their determined attacks a stronger force was needed. The Eastern Force withdrew back into the city under increasingly heavy enemy artillery fire.

Return to the **Keizer Karel Plein** and take the **Nassau Single** and the **Kronenburgers Single**. Note the public gardens of **Kronenburg Park** on the right. At the T-junction, in the square, **turn left** and go through the **railway underpass**. Look for a parking place.

Meanwhile, the Western Force set off under command of Captain JW Neville from its FUP to the south-west of the town. He recorded how:

'Our party had been given a guide, a Dutchman who spoke very little English. Nevertheless... we were able to reach our goal, which otherwise would have proved extremely difficult. The paratroopers rode on the backs of the tanks and we set off with the infantry carriers disposed between the tanks, keeping about 40 – 50 yards between each vehicle. I myself rode in the middle, giving instructions concerning the route on the wireless. The route went way out to the west with the result that the Railway Bridge was approached from its western side. To begin with, the advance was comparatively uneventful, with occasional shots from buildings. The principal trouble came from a house in which there were several Spandaus but these were knocked out with the 75mm from the leading tank. At this stage we expected the opposition to increase, but it would appear that they were in isolated houses, for the last 400 or 500 yards before

Nijmegen Railway Bridge 1943.

we reached the railway line were comparatively uneventful. No doubt, the Dutch guide had some part to play in this result.'

The encounter with the German outpost had fully alerted the enemy and Captain Neville reported looking back at a crossroads that they had just passed and seeing a German tank heading for what was obviously their last reported position. Meanwhile, a recce of the railway bridge's southern

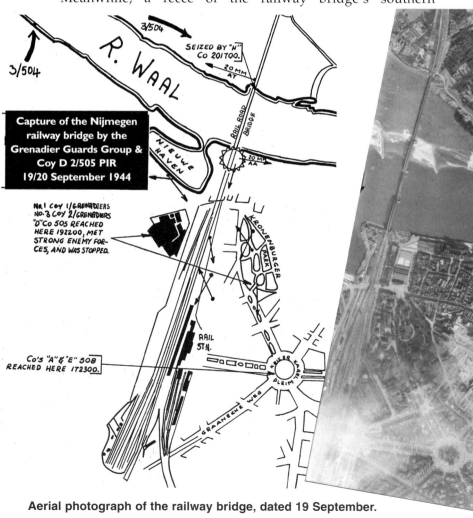

Aerial photograph of the railway bridge, dated 19 September.

embankment revealed that it was strongly defended, wi
mutually supporting machine and anti-tank guns. Captair
Neville continued:

'As the light was beginning to fade, we decided upon an
immediate attack. The plan was simple, if unimaginative. Three
tanks were to charge the opening in the embankment while the
other two gave covering fire. At the same time the Americans
aided by the infantry carriers, were to gain the embankment to
the south and drive out the machine-gunners from the flank.
Alas, the plan did not work. As soon as the leading tanks moved
forward across the open space, they came under heavy artillery
fire from a battery on the north bank of the Waal. Clearly, these
guns had been calibrated in advance. The leading tank was hit
and destroyed immediately, and the next was hit immediately
afterwards. All but one of the crew in the leading tank were killed
and my own driver, contrary to orders and with misplaced
bravery, jumped out of my tank and went to the rescue of those
trapped. The result was that the two crews were rescued but my
driver sustained serious burns. Our attack had lost impetus and
the lot of the Americans was no better. They came under
exceedingly heavy machine-gun fire, not only from the
embankment in front but also from Germans who were by then
on all sides. The Germans also had the support of two self-
propelled guns, which appeared through the tunnel in the
embankment and were engaged by our tanks. By this time it was
dark, and since we had failed to make any impression on the
defences, I decided to call off the attack during the night.

We withdrew about 100 yards and commandeered several
houses for a temporary headquarters. There were about six
seriously wounded men who probably would not have survived
without medical treatment. I decided to send back in a carrier.
The Americans, despite the reverse and a few casualties, were
still quite unmoved. We placed our three remaining tanks in
strategic places and everyone else took cover in the adjoining
houses. The American commander, who was otherwise a most
co-operative man, refused at this stage to have anything to do
with sentries, on the grounds that his men needed "a good
night's sleep" [they had had virtually no sleep for three
days]. Despite some forceful words from me, he remained
adamant. To protect themselves against surprise attack, their so-
called 'sentries' slept behind the doors so that any intruder

A Sherman Firefly of the Guards Armoured Division in the centre of Nijmegen.

> *would have to wake them up before getting in. My own expectation was, that we would be rushed during the night; and at frequent intervals we could hear the Germans moving around us.'*

The Allies had been fought to a standstill and it was to be over twelve hours before the next attack could be mounted.

A jeep of the US 82nd Airborne Division, transports a wounded soldier for treatment in Nijmegen.

CHAPTER EIGHT

CAPTURE OF THE WAAL BRIDGES

Evening – Tuesday 19 September 1944
Without any good news from Nijmegen Lieutenant Generals
Horrocks and Browning met at their co-located headquarters at
Malden. Just outside the city, General Horrocks recorded how:

'Suddenly the door opened and in came a tall, good-looking
American General, who like Maxwell Taylor commander of the
101st Airborne Division, was as unlike the popular [British]
cartoon conception of the loud-voiced, boastful, cigar-chewing
American as it would be possible to imagine. They were both
quiet, sensitive-looking men with an almost British passion for
understatement. Yet, both of these two commanders, under their
deceptively gentle exteriors, were very tough characters indeed.

**Horrocks to
Gavin:**

*'Jim, never
try to fight a
Corps off a
single road'.*

We pointed out to Jim Gavin that attacks on the road and
railway bridges in the town were making very slow progress and
that it was absolutely vital that both should, if possible, be
captured intact – though we could see that they were heavily
defended and had been prepared for demolition.'

General Gavin has recorded his response to the situation and his
orders:

'It seemed to me that the hour was becoming desperate.
Urquhart [1st Airborne Division] *had now been cut off for*
three days, and I still did not have the big Nijmegen bridge. If I
did nothing more than pour infantry and British armour into the
battle at our end of the bridge, we could be fighting there for days
and Urquhart would be lost. I decided therefore that I somehow
had to get across the river with our infantry and attack the
northern end of the bridge and cut the Germans off at the
southern end. ... I asked General Horrocks about boats, and he
said he thought they had some boats well down the road in the
train somewhere. The discussion on this point quickly spread
amongst the staff. They finally agreed that they should have
about twenty-eight folding canvas boats in trucks somewhere
farther to the rear. American boats, with which I was familiar,
were plywood, but at that moment boats were boats and I had to
have them.'

There were in fact thirty-two British assault boats available in the Guards Armoured Division's Engineer Field Park Squadron, however, this number was reduced to twenty-six when a truck carrying six boats was destroyed on Hell's Highway.

Wednesday 20 September 1944

General Gavin had a lot to think about as he drove the short distance up the hill to his CP. His divisional staff certainly had another sleepless night ahead of them, as they fleshed out the plan and issued orders.

'Back at Divisional Headquarters, we poured over the maps. [3/504PIR were to carry out an assault crossing]... In the meantime, every artillery piece, every tank gun, and every weapon we had would pour fire into the German positions on the far side. This would include as much smoke as we could get our hands on to cover the crossing. It was a risky tactic, but something had to be done. I could not conceive of sitting on the southern bank with a regiment of infantry and the Guards Armoured Division while Urquhart was destroyed eleven miles away.'

The second, and equally important part of the plan, was the renewed attack on the southern end of the bridges. If the Guards and 2/505 PIR were not equally successful, then the 504th would be destroyed in detail on the Island. This was a risk that General Gavin was prepared to take. Following the failure of the previous day's armoured and infantry charges towards the bridges, General Allan Adair planned a systematic clearance of Nijmegen that, in the words of the Guards' divisional history:

'would start at dawn the following morning [Wednesday 20 September], *preparatory to a major attack on the bridges fully supported by artillery later in the day; the risk of the Germans blowing them up in the meantime was fully appreciated, but there was no alternative. ... 5th Guards Brigade therefore assumed responsibility, with one American battalion* [2/505 PIR] *still under command, for clearing Nijmegen prior to seizing the bridges. This freed the 504th US Parachute Regiment to undertake the assault crossing, supported by two squadrons of 2nd Bn Irish Guards.'*

While the Allies were completing the planning of their attacks on the Waal crossings, shortly after dawn, 20 September, enemy pressure began mounting on the 82nd from the south. As has been explained the 82nd occupied thinly held positions on the

Grenadiers of 1st (Motorized) Battalion, Grenadier Guards, prepare for battle in the western part of Nijmegen.

Groesbeek Heights, covering what was, in effect, the Division's rear. Further back down Hell's Highway, 107th Panzer Brigade had renewed its attack on the bridge at Son, which was held by 101 Airborne Division, and closed it to Allied traffic. As the climax of the Nijmegen battle was approaching, the overall MARKET GARDEN situation was extremely unfavourable for the Allies.

The Capture of the Railway Bridge's Southern End – Afternoon, Wednesday 20 September 1944

The action on 20 September can best be viewed by going back under the railway bridge, and parking in **Joris Ivensplein** (not a part of town for the faint hearted to dally – it's a red light district) and walking to **Kronenburger Park**. The houses along the **Kronenburger Single** were where the Americans fought on the upper floor supported by British tanks on the road below.

As planned, the clearance of Nijmegen began at 08.30 hours on 20 September, under the Grenadiers' CO, Lieutenant Colonel Gouldburn. Their aim was:

> 'to clear enough of the town to have room to manoeuvre for

145

the final attack on the bridge itself, and also to make sure that the attack would not be molested by Germans advancing from the west.

'The attack went surprisingly well' with company / squadron groups of Grenadier Guards infantry or American paratroopers, supported by Grenadier tanks. Each was given a sector of the city to clear. The clearance was methodical, with a company of infantry clearing a block with a second company waiting behind them ready to clear the next block once the first had broken any resistance. Initially, the Germans, were content to inflict any delay they could on the advancing Allies and then fell back towards the main positions, occupying an area about three hundred metres deep and about 1,000 metres long covering the bridges.'

The force heading for the railway bridge closed in quickly on the enemy's main defences around the embankment leading up to the bridge. They had taken a route to the east; the opposite side of the railway line to their previous attempt. However, Company D, 2/505 and Grenadier tanks became bogged down as they attempted to cross the open fields of fire in the Kronenburger Park. *Kampfgruppe* Henke with a stiffening of SS

Fitters from the Royal Electrical and Mechanical Engineers work on a Grenadiers' tank damaged during the street fighting in Nijmegen.

troops was standing firm and the advance slowed as buildings surrounding the park had to be cleared room by room. During the course of the battle General Gavin went forward into Nijmegen to see for himself how 2/505 and their Grenadier Guards tanks were getting-on in the west of the city:

'... but there was little to be seen, since most of the fighting was taking place in the buildings and on the rooftops. Later the veteran troopers told me about the experience. What they wanted to do, they said, was ... fire down into the gun positions of the 88s and the foxholes of the Germans. This they eventually did. It was a new experience for the troopers, but they soon discovered that the best technique was to fight from rooftop to rooftop; thus, they were always on high ground. Where necessary, they blew holes in the upper floors of adjoining buildings so as to make their way forward and still be on top of the Germans.'

A Grenadier Guards officer later described the action of 2/505 PIR to General Gavin as 'A jolly sight to see those paratroopers hopping from rooftop to rooftop'.

Meanwhile, on the other side of the river, SS-*Sturmbannführer* Reinhold, the Nijmegen garrison commander, was visited by his divisional commander and briefed on the progress of the battle. He was told about the increasing Allied resources being concentrated on Nijmegen, despite the seven battalion attack on Mook and Groesbeek mounted by General Eugen Meindl's II *Fallschirmjäger* Corps. These German attacks had been designed to divert the Allies from the bridges to the still thinly held positions on the Groesbeek Heights. In this, they were unsuccessful but they were diverting the Allies reserves away from Nijmegen. This lack of reserves in Nijmegen was to have an important impact on the outcome of MARKET GARDEN.

The Assault River Crossing – 15.00 Hours Wednesday 20 September 1944

Return to your car. It is not normally possible to reach the riverbank where 3/504 crossed from or where the fire support group took up position, as the location is an industrial area. An excellent view of the crossing site, from the German viewpoint is included later in the tour. For those who wish to visit the general area, go back through the underpass and follow **Voorstadslaan** from the area of the railway bridge and turn right onto **Weurtse Weg**. Follow this road for a mile and turn right onto the **Winselingsweg**. This area is still occupied by a modern power station and factories. This is the area where the troops assembled and the attack was launched.

Early on the morning of 20 September 1944, Lieutenant John Holabird, 307 Engineers, of 504 PIR was amongst the first to

view the river that the Allied generals' had decided, in some desperation, that they were to cross:

'C Company, 307th Engineers had moved closer to the river. Captain "Spike" Harris called me and together we walked up the power station on the Waal River with other C Company officers and platoon sergeants. I had no idea why we were going. We met with Colonel Tucker [CO 504th Parachute Infantry Regiment], *Major Cook and other field grade officers. I was sure something BIG was going on because ordinarily we wouldn't have been party to all those upper ranks of officers. We walked upstairs in the empty power station and looked out over the river, it was broad. ... About then I began to understand what was up. We were going to cross it and the Engineers in the U.S. Army were the customary boatmen. Ergo, we were there to plot a night crossing. "Where were the boats?" we asked. "Coming," they replied. "What kind of boats?" "Press out, British canvas assault boats." "How soon?" "Afternoon." And then I began to understand that they were really serious about a daylight crossing. Wow! "Who's going to protect us? That is one wide river." – "We'll lay in British armour to hit the other side and to lay down a smoke barrage so no one will be able to see." It began to dawn on me that this was one rash daredevil idea and we engineers were going to be a big part of it. We went back to the company and we moved up in enfilade to the east of the power station on the down* [inland] *side of the levee or embankment.'*

Major Cook of 504 Parachute Infantry Regiment.

Colonel Ruben Tucker's 504 PIR had been relieved by the Welsh Guards, who took over defence of the Grave area. The plan was for 3/504 PIR to conduct the assault across the river, followed by the 1st Battalion. The 2nd Battalion was to clear the area surrounding the power station and provide fire support. 504 PIR had moved towards the western suburbs of Nijmegen in time for an H Hour of 08.00 hours but this was delayed to 11.00, then to 13.30 and eventually to 15.00 hours. General Horrocks describes the frustration:

'... owing to the difficulty of getting lorries containing the boats up the one long narrow road which constituted our lines of communication and which, in spite of all our efforts, was from time to time completely blocked by burnt-out vehicles. The delay in getting these precious boats forward was infuriating, and it was the only time that I saw Gavin really angry. Having flown in he did not understand the chaotic situation at ground level in the rear, and as Zero Hour for the crossing had to be constantly postponed, he turned to me and said, "For God's sake try! It's the least you can do".'

Meanwhile, Captain Moffatt Burriss, commander of Company I 3/504 PIR, sheltering behind the river embankment, said:

'We were not shown the river before the crossing. We waited the other side of the levee most of the day. If we had seen what we were expected to cross in daylight, we probably wouldn't have done it! I still wonder how any of us survived the crossing.'

Lieutenant Thomas Pitt recalls how his battalion:

'was selected to be the guinea pigs. So the first thing that was to occur prior to the actual crossing was that we were to get some air cover. British Spitfires [Typhoons] that had long range capability were operating out of France. Finally after some delay, two spitfires [sic] came over and started to strafe the opposite banks and on the opposite dike where the Krauts were dug-in. About the second pass, the Germans got one of the Spitfires and the other one went home. So that was the end of the air cover.

Lieutenant Thomas Pitt.

The British had these large tanks; I forget the name of it [Shermans]. They were going to give us some artillery fire but first laid down some smoke. There were about some eight or ten of them [tanks] that dug in up closer to the bridge from us. They opened fire and they put a lot of iron down in a short period, but in a couple of minutes the [German] counter battery came.'

In fact, Lieutenant Pitt has seen only a part of the direct fire support available. The Irish Guards' history describes their part in the successful crossing:

'*Colonel Giles* [Vandeleur] *took Major DRS FitzGerald and the troop commanders forward on foot to choose fire positions for the tanks. The timings had to be calculated exactly as the whole area was more or less under German observation and was already under spasmodic shell fire. ... At half-past two the tanks moved slowly up to the river, reaching their positions just before three. No. 2 Squadron lined the embankment near the Power House and No. 3 Squadron hid behind rubble heaps on the waste land round the factory. No. 2 Squadron had by far the better field of fire, but was itself completely exposed to the Germans on the far bank. ...Fortunately* [most of] *the German 88mm and 20mm guns had been sited for anti-aircraft work and so, not being able to depress their barrels low enough to fire into the river, concentrating on the Irish Guards' tanks.'*

In addition to the tanks the combined artillery of the 82nd and Guards Armoured Divisions, totalling approximately one hundred field guns, fired in support. They had been in action through out the day in support of the Grenadiers and 2/505 in Nijmegen as they closed in on the enemy's main defences around the bridges. Only one supply convoy had reached the Guards Armoured and the 82nd's artillery supply arrangements had failed. Therefore, ammunition was strictly limited but most

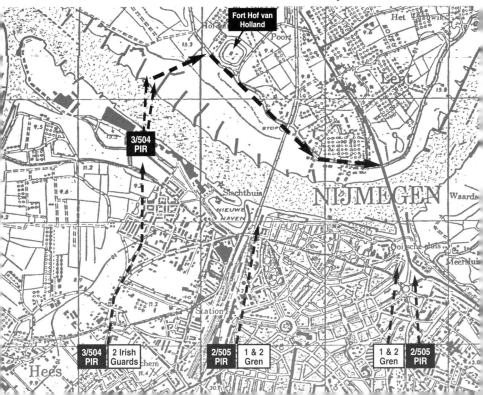

guns had approximately fifty rounds each, plus, in some cases, a few extras dumped on the gun positions. It was very different from the experience of Normandy, when artillery ammunition was virtually always available, and fired, in seemingly limitless quantities. Nonetheless, the desperate need to get across the Waal and on to the Rhine led to a decision to risk running artillery ammunition down to dangerously low levels. Even so the artillery had only enough ammunition to engage immediate targets. The lack of artillery ammunition was to have a greatly underestimated effect on XXX Corps' conduct of the remainder of MARKET GARDEN and artillery ammunition was not restored to normal until final clearing of Hell's Highway on 26 September 1944.

The fire-plan began shortly before 15.00 hours with a heavy smoke screen, as 3/504 PIR dashed over the river embankment. The main armament and machine-guns of the Irish Guards supplemented the artillery and mortar fire. Using vital tank ammunition to cover 3/504 PIR's crossing, severely limited the options open to General Adair, later that day.

The assault route taken by the (US) 3/504 over the river Waal 20 September.

The crossing of the Waal by the Paratroopers of the 3/504 on the afternoon of 20 September 1944, as depicted at the Groesbeek Museum.

Lieutenant Pitt continues his infantryman's eye view of the crossing:

'The boat was like a canvas material with a wood frame to it and it held about twelve men in a boat. We had to paddle to get it across. We took the boats and came from behind the factory (I don't think the Krauts knew we were there). We started down across the sandy shore which was maybe 50 yards long till we got to the water. We were running with these boats and our weapons and what not. In addition to all that crap the old man [the CO, Major Cook] said you lay a telephone line across the river so we can talk back to them, if we need support fire or something. We weren't sure that the radios would work that distance with the one's we had. So I had a kid from the communications section join us with a roll of wire on a spindle-like thing.

'We got into the damn boats and thought it at first it looked like rain in the water. Then we realized it was lead coming from the Krauts on the other side and away we went. I'll tell you we

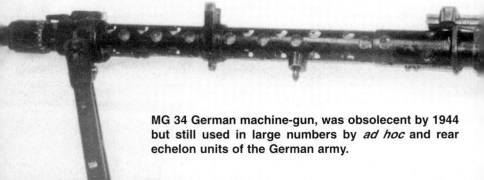

MG 34 German machine-gun, was obsolecent by 1944 but still used in large numbers by *ad hoc* and rear echelon units of the German army.

were paddling like mad to get across. Quite a few of the boats overturned; guys in a lot of them were killed in getting across the river. I don't know how many boats we had lost in the river. It was a hell of a wide river [175 yards].'

Engineer Lieutenant John Holabird, also recalls the crossing and how after the command 'Go':

'We sprang into action. After all, we were the so-called "river crossing experts." We hauled the boats down one by one. Did we figure out to press them out, or did some Brit show us? Who knows? Anyhow, we got one opened up. Was there a command to move out? I can't remember. I just knew we were supposed to crack this boat down the embankment across the sandy shore and across the river. How did I feel? I was numb and frozen. But I figured that if Spike and the big shots thought we could make it, why not?

I rallied my squad; grabbed the boat and headed down the embankment about 15 feet. I think the canvas boat was heavier than it looked – then across sandy mud to the river's edge and into the water. We pushed the boat out to where we could all step in. All hell was breaking loose. Tanks firing smoke and lots of small arms fire. I had experience with canoes and rowboats, plus a period on a freshman crew at Harvard. So I took the stern and shouted, "stroke!" – "stroke!" – "stroke!" as we wallowed across the Waal.'

Captain Moffatt Burris was waiting with his company in the dead ground behind the dyke listening to the fire support reach a crescendo.

'As we came out into the open, the weight of our boat seemed imponderable; our feet sank deep into the mud. We must have caught the krauts by surprise, because for the first 100 yards there wasn't a round fired from the enemy side of the river. Then suddenly all hell broke loose. We had run halfway across the flat topped plateau prior to reaching the drop, when Jerry opened up

The Waal in 1944.

with everything he had – LMGs, Mortars, 20mm guns, artillery and rifles. As if in a rage at our trying anything so dangerous, he was throwing everything he owned at us.

At last we reached the drop. We let our boats slide down to the beach and we ourselves slid alongside them. We pulled our boat quickly across the short beach, and everyone piled in. By this time, the situation was horrible. The automatic fire had increased and the artillery was deadly. Men were falling to the right and left of me. Our ears were filled with the constant roar of bursting artillery shells, the dull wham of a 20-mm round or the disconcerting ping of rifle bullets.

Men grabbed paddles and started frantically to work. Most of the men had not paddled before; and had it not been for the gruesomeness of the situation, the sight might have been ludicrous. With all our strength, we would lunge forward only to miss the water completely. Gradually our boat got moving in the right direction. We lunged forward at different times.

.... Occasionally I lifted my head to give directions to the engineer steering our boat and to cast a cursory glance at the other 25 boats. By now the Waal was covered with our small canvas craft, all crammed with frantically paddling men. ... Large numbers of men were being hit in all boats, and the bottoms of these craft were littered with the wounded and the dead. Here and there on the surface of the water there floated a paddle dropped by some poor casualty before the man taking his place could retrieve it from lifeless fingers.

The water all around the boats was churned up by the hail of bullets, and we were soaked to the skin. Out of the corner of my

154

eye, I saw a boat hit in the middle by a 20-mm shell and sink. Somewhere on my left, I caught a glimpse of a figure topple overboard, only to be grabbed and pulled back on board by some hardy soul.

We were soaked, gasping for breath, dead tired, and constantly expecting to feel that searing sensation as the bullet tore through you. I wanted to vomit. Many did. Somehow or other we were three-fourths of the way across. Everyone was yelling to keep it up but there was little strength left in anyone. ... But at last we reached the other side.

We climbed over the wounded and the dead in the bottom of the boat and – up to our knees in water – waded to shore.'

General Gavin was now at the division's rear near Mook, dealing with a crisis there. However, it seemed that any one of any importance was observing 504 PIR's crossing from the power station roof. The reaction of the watching senior British officers was of incredulity -*'Unbelievable!'* Typical comments were, *'My God, what a courageous sight it was.'* by Lieutenant Colonel J.O.E Vandeleur and *'I have never seen a more gallant action'* was the crisp comment from General Browning.

Across the river the Germans had been caught by surprise, Heinz Harmel, commander of *Kampfgruppe* Frundsberg said *'Crossing one of Europe's widest and fast flowing rivers in daylight was inconceivable and dismissed as suicidal.'* Consequently, he had only deployed outposts along the dyke road, about six hundred yards from the riverbank. However, fire trenches dug into the dyke dominated the flat and open land that the Americans had to cross and against even a lightly held screen, the attack was to be costly. Allied fire was concentrated on the dyke; particularly the Irish Guards' tank machine guns.

Having reached the narrow river beach 3/504 charged over the flat flood plain towards the dyke. Captain Moffat Burriss recalls how *'I was angry and we charged across the open flood land without stopping'*. This was achieved with the support of concentrated covering fire and smoke. The smoke was not entirely effective and a 20mm anti-aircraft gun on the railway bridge's northern embankment was soon in action but it was unable to stop the madly charging paratroopers. Infantryman Lieutenant Thomas Pitt recalls:

'We were coming across another beach-like area 600 yards wide before the final dike. They were dug-in some on the beach

and then back in the dike. We were running by them and they were just shooting. The only thing to do was to head for the dike because there wasn't a Goddamed bit of cover anywhere else or anything. So we finally got about half way back to the dike and this kid who is peeling off this wire and he says "I ran out of wire should I set the phone up here?" I said "hell with it kid just take it easy now and get to the dike. We will talk to them some other day." So we finally got over to the dike. The Krauts on the other side. The dike must have been maybe ten yards or so wide at the top and they were on the backside. We spent a little time tossing grenades from one side or the other – that was fun and games. They were there with their potato mashers and we had fragmentation grenades. My job was to hold the left flank so as we moved down towards the bridge the Krauts wouldn't turn and come behind us. So, we proceeded to hold it [the dike]. The Krauts tried to come across a couple times.'

Following the initial assault, 1/504 PIR was crossing the fire swept river in a steadily reducing number of boats. Ahead of them, at 16.45 hours, HQ 504 PIR reported to divisional headquarters that they were '...across the river and 3/504 were advancing against the enemy' bridges to their east. Lieutenant John Holabird and his engineers mission was to accompany the infantry and destroy as many German demolition circuits as he could on the two bridges. He recalls that:

'We scampered out of the boats and up the beach to higher ground and took off gradually east where we knew the highway bridge to be. We were eight young men, who had just won a new life and we dashed like a cavalry squadron. Nothing could stop us now and we didn't wait for the 504th. There was a pillbox in front of us. Who knows if there were any defenders? We tossed in grenades and shot ahead. There were two houses. I think uninhabited but we tossed grenades there too and romped on. At some point I bethought me of duties as an officer, wrote a brief, and sent it back by one of my engineers.

We spread out. From here on I get hazy. I was down to six and we were hooping and hollering all over the place. Like a bad officer, I got ahead of the group. I remember running through a large pasture; was surprised by the whistling of bullets going by; wondering if someone was really trying to shoot at me, me, the victorious crosser of the Waal. Finally, after an hour and a half, my euphoria began to wane. I took off my helmet and looked around. It must have been 5 or 5:30 by this time. Bullets still whistling around – but presumably not at me (I hoped) – I wondered what in the world I should be doing? No men, no mission, not really an infantryman. Two of my men arrived and we took council and wondered whether to proceed or get back to the beachhead.

At this point, we discovered Major Cook and elements of the 3rd Battalion coming towards us in a ditch. I reported in to Major Cook, told him that everything was OK this far and since I had only two of my squad left, I probably should see what I could do at the landing.'

Back at the crossing point, which was still under fire, 504 PIR was still being paddled across the Waal to expand the bridgehead to the north and north-west. At the same time, the British 615 Field Squadron Royal Engineers, under heavy artillery and mortar fire, were ferrying American equipment, such as anti-tank guns and mortars, across the river. These heavy weapons were essential if 504 PIR was to repel the inevitable German counter-attacks.

Hof van Holland – Afternoon – Wednesday 20 September 1944

Five hundred metres to the west of the railway bridge lay a 17th Century fortification, of high earthen banks surrounded by a wide, water-filled, moat, called Fort Lent or Hof van Holland. The Allied tactical planning map prepared on 11 September 1944, showed at least one 88 mm and the presence of a section of 81mm mortars. From the cover of the fort, the mortars could provide fire support to any part of the Germans defences in Nijmegen. However, nine days later the fort had been reinforced by SS infantry, with their usual high proportion of *Spandaus*. Colonel Tucker, commander 504 PIR, recalls how, having watched the crossing from the power station, he:

Colonel Tucker

'... came down and jumped into one of the boats with my G-3 [operations staff officer] and went across the river to arrive just as grenades and fire were brought down on Fort Lent.'

Communications were working well back to the fire support group on the southern bank of the Waal, despite the mixing of troops and confusion inherent in battle. Indirect fire had stunned the defenders. Colonel Tucker arrived just as fire from Allied

mortars and artillery lifted and, in the words of the historian of the Irish Guards the fort received

> '... *particular attention – even armour piercing shot to keep the defenders' heads down'.*

The American paratroopers closed in for yet another spectacular kill. Colonel Tucker continued:

> '*What happened – there was grenade and mortar fire into the fort area, then a running dive into the moat. The bridge into the fort was kept clear by riflemen who fired at anything that moved. I went into the fort behind the initial troops.'*

A deadly blend of clinical military efficiency and raw courage had overcome a strong position, covering approaches to the railway bridge. So it was, that small groups of determined Americans reached the northern end of the railway bridges, driven on by the 'intoxication of the crossing'. In the words of XXX Corps' historian:

> '*By six o'clock the American flag was seen to be flying on the northern end of the railway bridge. This magnificent assault is probably one of the most amazing achievements of the war, and it could have been carried out only by a very fine division.'*

The Capture of the Railway Bridge – Late Afternoon 20 September 1944

Captain Neville and a part of his mixed group of Grenadiers and paratroopers penetrated the enemy positions on the railway bridge's southern embankment, while the remainder of his force was held up by the SS at the Kronenburger Park. Guardsman Howe, who had been so pleased to ride into Nijmegen in one of his battalion's Bren Gun Carriers on 19 September, recalls the fighting:

> '*After our battle the day before, we were a bit short of ammunition but I had a satchel of grenades that I used clearing the enemy out of the houses he had occupied between our positions and the railway bridge. The day seemed to go on forever. Grenades through windows or door. The crack of the detonation and in we went with a burst from the Bren and the bayonet. The strange thing is that throughout the whole battle I never saw a live German until I reached the bridge and they were running away across it.'*

However, elsewhere, as the Grenadiers reported,

> '*The SS and young troops fought savagely, but the old men*

Nijmegen rail Bridge

ARNHEM →

The original underpass on the Ousterhout Dyke road. Note the pill box which had excellent fields of fire.

ran away or surrendered when the SS soldiers' backs were turned'.

By early afternoon, the Allies' hold on the southern end of the railway bridge was still tenuous, with fighting in the surrounding streets and houses. Captain Neville was unable to report his Company Squadron group's success to the Grenadiers' Headquarters, as his radio was suffering the same problems of screening, as those experienced by the 1st Airborne Division in the streets of Arnhem. If he had been able to report, perhaps the Grenadiers' main effort could have been switched to the railway bridge and the success exploited far more quickly. All German accounts are definite in that they lost control of the southern end of the bridge mid-afternoon but most Allied accounts based on divisional level war diaries paint a far less clear picture. However what is clear is that elements of 3/504

The railway bridge was badly damaged by German frogmen on September 1944 and was rebuilt after the war. The modern concrete stands on the original stone piers.

NIJMEGEN

PIR were established at the northern end of the railway bridge by early evening. Private Albert Tarbel, company radio operator, recorded in his diary:

'After fighting with different groups from our H Company, I was trying to rejoin Captain Kappel. I finally met with him at the railroad bridge. We also had quite a fight there. At one point, we were passing Gammon grenades to Captain Kappel, who was throwing them at the German soldiers through an opening in the northern bridge tower entrance. Needles to say, we neither offered nor gave any quarter to the Germans on the railroad bridge.'

Lieutenant Keep, of Company I, writing shortly after the event, describes how, once the railway bridge was secure how they:

'...organized defences, knowing the Krauts would counterattack to get it back. We heard rumours that German tanks were coming from one direction, infantry from another. However, we did face fanatics who constantly crept towards us from the middle of the great bridge, coming as close as they dared, then throwing potato mashers [stick grenades]. *It was suicide, but such individuals are ever prevalent among the present-day representatives of the Herrenvolk* [master race].

Then at dusk, a strange thing happened. Out of the darkness loomed a tremendous mass of German soldiers walking from the middle of the bridge and approaching our end. There must have been 200 – 300 of them. We all thought our goose was cooked and were prepared to open up with what small firepower we had left when one of the Krauts called in German that they wanted to surrender. ... Had they realized what a paltry group we were, I fear all thoughts of surrender would have vanished and they would have turned bellicose.'

Sadly, word that the railway bridge was taken did not strike home in the minds of the divisional staffs, as British and American attention was focused on the fight for the Road Bridge.

The Attack on the Road Bridge – Afternoon and Early Evening Wednesday 20 September 1944

Return via the railway bridge and **Keizer Karel Plein**, on to the **Oranje Single**. Follow the road, on to the open **Keizer Traianus Plein** (formerly known as Kaiser Lodwijk Plein). The road system is complicated but follow signs to '**Centrum and Parking**'. Turn on to **St Joris Straat** and look for a parking space. On most days of the week, the best thing to do is to park in the **underground car park** that has its entrance as the square opens out. The modern museum dominating the **Kelfkensbosch** square does not contain material relating to 1944 but stands on the site of buildings that contained SS-*Hauptsturmführer* Euling's battalion headquarters (see page 169). From the car park, a short walk around the **Valkhof Gardens** and **Hunner Park** will take the visitor to the scene of the action on 20 September 1944.

Starting at 08.00 hours, Lieutenant Prescott, commanding a troop of Shermans from No.2 Squadron 2/Grenadier Guards, was to clear the main road from Keizer Karel Plein to the bridge:

'*Initially I was placed under command of 4 Company of the 1st Battalion and our task was to clear the main street from the "ring road"*[Oranje Single] *up to the Valkhof Gardens overlooking the bridge. I married up with the infantry company south of the ring road and we soon set off across this road. I recall seeing American parachutists dug in along the road in verge between the two carriageways. One could not but get the impression that they were very tired. We made reasonably good progress down the street with the infantry clearing the houses, while the tank troops, of necessity on a one-tank front, gave fire support up at the windows. I recall coming under small arms fire at one time and having to close down, and shortly afterwards*

The view of the bridge from the German pill box on the Valkhof.

VELORAMA

having mortar fire directed onto my tank and closing down once more. My troop corporal was shot through the arm while in the cupola of his tank, but was able to continue in command. We reached the open square Kelfkenbosch in front of Valkhof Gardens and stopped to take stock.'

This phase of the operation took about five hours. The American paratroopers, along with the Grenadiers' tanks and infantry steadily closed in on the bridge, clearing houses as they went. SS-*Hauptsturmfuhrer* Schwappacher recorded in his after action report:

'Whenever the enemy was ready to advance on the bridge we hit him with the full impact of an artillery barrage, which immediately halted the attacks, whereupon our infantry, reinforced, were able to maintain their positions.'

Despite the considerable strength of the *Frundsberg's* artillery, the mounting Allied pressure and losses eventually forced the SS soldiers to start pulling back from the southern edge of Hunner Park to positions on the western side of the Arnhemsche Weg. However, the road to the bridge that the Allies sought so desperately was covered by enemy fire. The burning hulks of Shermans that had previously fought their way onto the approach to the bridge, were a testimony to the effectiveness of the *Panzerfaust* in the hands of determined soldiers.

Having reached the Kelfkensbosch Square on the southern edge of Hunner Park and the Valkhof Gardens, the Allies were forced to pause to regroup and re-supply for the final assault on the main enemy positions guarding the road bridge. The plan that Lieutenant Colonels Goulburn and Vandervoort agreed was that the Grenadier infantry would assault Hunner Park and the Valkhof, while Vandervoort's 2/505 PIR would attack enemy positions on the northern edge of the Kaizer Lodewijk roundabout. H Hour for all three attacks was set at 15.30 hours, half an hour after 3/504 PIR eventually started their much delayed assault river crossing.

1/Grenadiers were to assault the Valkhof Gardens from the area of the Police Station, to the west, with King's Company, reinforced by Lieutenant Dawson's Platoon from No. 2 Company. No. 4 Company was to cross the open Kelfkenbosch/St Joris Straat square and clear the Hunner Park and capture the Belvedere. No. 2 and No. 3 Companies were to

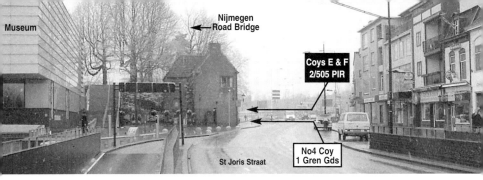

A view from the open Kelfkensbosch through St Joris Straat to the Kaiser Lodewik Plein.

cover the flanks of the assaulting companies and provide reserves if necessary. The tanks of 2/Grenadiers would remain divided up in support of the British infantry and the American paratroopers. The attack was delivered with only the sketchiest orders to platoon commanders. However, this was of little consequence as one company commander explained:

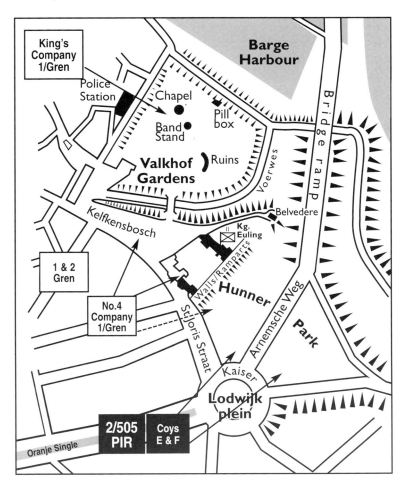

SS-*Hauptsturmführer* Karl-Heinz Euling.

'From the first five minutes, the fighting did not conform in any way to my original plan, but once we got our teeth into the enemy the men's spirit was so terrific – even laughing and joking that nothing could have stopped us.'

Facing a dangerous enemy, such as soldiers of the *Waffen SS*, this light-hearted reaction to the likelihood of sudden, violent death was familiar to the seasoned commanders.

The Germans' main positions around the bridge were still held by soldiers of SS-*Hauptsturmführer* Euling's battalion, along with those from the outposts, who had fallen back to join their comrades. In addition, two weak companies of SS engineers under SS-*Untersturmführer* Wener Baumgaertel held strong points in the centre of the Valkhof Gardens, and in the Belvedere which provided the German position some depth to its defences. The whole area was festooned with barbed wire entanglements and a complex of shallow crawl trenches dug over the preceeding days as reinforcements had arrived. At this time, four of the *Frundsberg's*

A rare surviving Resistance document prepared in Nijmegen by Jan Van Hoof. He passed such information to the SOE in London March 1944. The shaded areas depict fortified buildings, which with the trench system, made the Valkhof an extremely strong position. The numbered triangles symbolise German pill boxes.

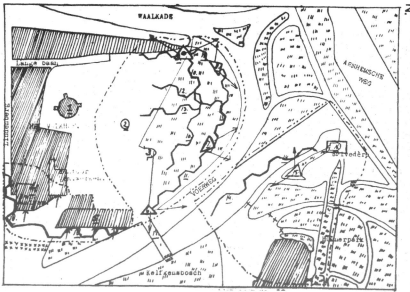

The Kelfkensbosch and the ornamental bridge into the Valkhof Gardens. Tanks of 2/Grenadiers were knocked out attempting to cross the square.

assault guns were still operational, with more covering the bridge's northern ramp.

The King's Company got off to a good start as the enemy were clearly not expecting a flank attack, with their main positions facing the open area of the Kelfkensbosch. This meant that the Guards were able to cut their way through the barbed wire entanglements and climb up a steep rubble slope to the western edge of the Valkhof Gardens. If the German had properly covered this obstacle with fire, the Guardsmen would have been unlikely to have broken into the main enemy position. However, even so casualties were high and King's Company lost its commander in this first phase of the battle. Lieutenant Dawson, who had arrived to join the attack, just as the advance began, took over command of King's Company in the absence of other officers. Lance Sergeant Simpson recalls:

'We reached the top of the slope and the platoons in the ruins

Looking down Lindenberg towards the Waal. King's Company 2/Grenadiers attacked from the Police station (now replaced) across the road and up the rubble covered slope into the Valkhof on the right.

POLICE
STATION

of the police station behind us were firing away over our heads. We paused to gain our breath and charge our magazines. We then dashed forward a short distance to a German trench. It wasn't very deep and led to positions to our right. Still it was good cover which was very welcome and I found that I had had close shave, with a round having shot through my water bottle on my hip.'

Having gained a toehold on the edge of the Valkhof with his two leading platoons, Lieutenant Dawson attempted to expand his lodgement by sending a reserve platoon around to the right under covering fire. Unfortunately this platoon lost heavily, as it ran into an SS position and had to withdraw. Lieutenant Dawson's second flanking attempt, this time on the left, was more successful. The platoon made its way under cover of the embankment to within fifty yards of the bridge but they were unable to reach it due to heavy Allied and German fire that was sweeping the area. Having retraced their route slightly, they were able to fight their way up into the Gardens behind the Germans. From this position, the platoon was able to the dominate the Valkhof area and bring fire down onto Hunner Park and the southern approaches to the bridge. This fire support was of considerable assistance to No.4 Company and Companies E and F of 2/505 PIR. Providing fire support to other attacks was easy but winkling determined SS defenders out of the Valkhof, was to be a protracted and nasty business.

No. 4 Company attacked Hunner Park across the

The route around the northern edge of the Valkhof Gardens (see Resistance map on previous page) taken by a platoon from King's Company.

Bridge

PILL BOX

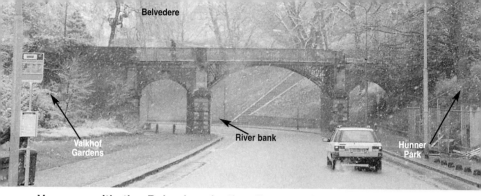

Belvedere

Valkhof Gardens — **River bank** — **Hunner Park**

Voreweg with the Belvedere in the distance. It formed a deep trench between the Valkhof Gardens and Hunner Park.

Kelfkensbosch, as the enemy had anticipated. They attacked on a two-platoon frontage but this time each platoon was supported by a Sherman tank. As the Grenadiers' regimental history describes, the attack did not get off to a good start:

> 'Lieutenant Fazackerly led off, fanning across the open ground. They had not advanced more than a hundred yards before the Germans opened up with the most withering fire from the area of the bridge. Lieutenant Fazackerly was shot through the stomach, Lieutenant Prescott's tank was hit by an enormous shell and blew up, Lance Sergeant Heawood and his section were mown down and pinned down by fire, and casualties started to mount all round at a most alarming rate.'

Major Stanley decided to move his company further to the right, as it was clearly impossible to cross the Kelfkensbosch. However, with the buildings along the southern side burning, re-deploying was not easy and very slow. Having reached the

The pill box built into the walls of the Valkhof. From here machine guns covered one of the approaches to the bridge.

The Chapel in the Valkhof Gardens was repaired after the war but its massive walls stood up to shot and shell remarkably well.

Americans on the St Joris Straat, No. 4 Company found the paratroopers similarly pinned down by Spandau fire from the Belvedere area and Keiser-Lodewijk Plein. St Joris Straat was much narrower at this point and the buildings across the fire swept road were obviously fortified but until these buildings were cleared, no progress towards the bridge could be made. The risk had to be taken.

Under covering fire from paratroopers and fellow Guardsmen, with mortars and tanks firing smoke the leading Allied platoons crossed the road and made their way through the gardens bordering the Hunner Park, towards the Belvedere. The regimental history describes how the leading platoon reached about thirty yards from:

> 'the fort. Lieutenant Greenall and his ten strong "platoon" immediately charged at it and succeeded in driving away the whole force of Germans, killing many of them and taking about thirty prisoners.'

This was a well-developed position, strongly held by SS engineers but news that the Americans had crossed the river behind them must have undermined their morale and contributed to the Guards' and Paratroopers' ascendancy. The Grenadiers' historian describes the action in the buildings between St Joris Straat and Valkhof:

> 'At the same time, Lieutenant Slob's Platoon surrounded a large house near by, covered the exits with machine-guns and threw in phosphorous grenades which roasted alive about 150

The Belvedere occupied by 10 SS Engineers and captured by 2/502 PIR. This view is from the Valkhof Gardens across Voerweg to the bridge's southern ramp.

Bridge

Germans who were inside. At this point all serious German resistance seemed to crack. They were overwhelmed by fire ... Soon a patrol from No. 4 Company moved down on to the bridge and, apart from a considerable quantity of shell-shocked prisoners, found it clear.'

The 'large house' was Haus Robert Jannssen, which SS-*Hauptsturmfuhrer* Euling used as his HQ and strong point. Euling escaped the fire and carnage in his headquarters as the Guardsmen and flames advanced on him. Leading sixty survivors of his battalion, he escaped down the steep bank into the Voerweg and to safety under the road bridge. (See dotted line on map).

A copy of SS-*Hauptsturmführer* Karl-Heinz Euling's map, showing his defence of the Nijmegen bridge.

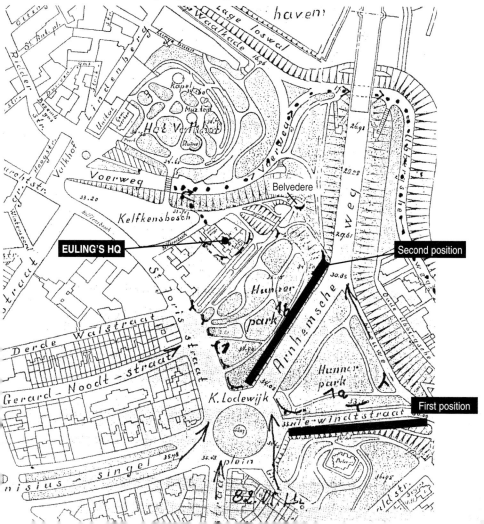

Hunner Park after the battle. A dead Guardsman surrounded by German equipment testifies to the severity of the fighting.

Meanwhile, Companies E and F, 2/505 had, with the addition of the Guards, assembled sufficient combat power for them to clear the Kaiser Lodewijk Plein Roundabout and the eastern portion of Hunner Park. The removal of the enemy from the Belvedere helped their advance considerably. The Grenadiers' tanks, with the advantage of numbers, won a deadly fight with the German assault guns. Even so, a tank advancing any distance into uncleared territory towards the bridge risked being knocked out by *Panzerfausts*.

In the gathering dusk, the bloody business of clearing enemy positions in detail began. This went on late into the night. So determined was the resistance by pockets of SS defenders, that it shaped the following day's battle. However, as daylight failed, the Allies had vital footholds on the southern approaches to both bridges. At divisional headquarters, realization that their troops had reached their objectives, coincided with a garbled radio message that the Americans of 504 PIR had *'reached the northern end of the Bridge'*. The Grenadiers could see nothing through thick smoke screens but the message galvanized 2/Grenadiers into taking a desperate risk. They were to launch another attempt to get tanks across the area littered with the burning hulks and bodies of those who had earlier led the way onto the Kaiser Lodewijk Plein and the road bridge beyond. However, the garbled message had referred to the rail bridge where the Stars and Stripes could indeed be seen not the road bridge. This mistake, of a type only too common in war, caused orders to be issued.

Return to your car and head for the **Keizer Traianus Plein** (formerly Kaiser Lodewijk Plein) and follow signs for **Arnhem**. This will take the visitor across the vital bridge. There is no stopping on the bridge and the driver should concentrate on the road rather than the view, as traffic moves quickly. **Take the first slip road off** the bridge's northern ramp signposted towards **Lent West**. **Turn left** along the dike road and after a hundred metres park in the first pull off. Just in front is the large concrete bunker from which SS *Brigadefuhrer* Heinz Harmel watched the final assault on the bridge.

The Grenadiers Rush the Bridge – 1900 Hours Wednesday 20 September 1944

The tanks of No. 1 Squadron 2/Grenadiers were the only uncommitted reserve in Nijmegen. The squadron commander, Major Trotter, himself having been briefed by Lieutenant

Nijmegen citizens look on as a Sherman belonging to 2/Grenadiers await orders to move towards the road bridge.

A Sherman belonging to 2/Grenadiers, prior to the assault on Nijmegen road bridge.

Colonel Goldburn, called his second in command Captain Lord Peter Carrington, and troop commander, Sergeant Peter Robinson, for orders outside the Nijmegen Hotel. Of the two reporting for orders, the former was a peer of the realm and wartime soldier, while the later was a hard bitten Regular Army Guardsman and one of the battalion's few non-officer troop commanders. Lord Carrington eventually became British Secretary of State for Defence and head of NATO. In one of his typically clear pieces of military thinking, Lord Carrington summed up the orders he and Sergeant Robinson had been given,

> *'We thought that someone must be round the bend, to order an assault on the bridges. They were certain to be mined, and would probably be blown up under us as we crossed. The orders were for Sergeant Robinson "to take the bridge at all costs" to enable us to link up with the American paratroops who had previously crossed the Waal approximately one mile west, and were believed to be clearing north of the bridge'.*

Lieutenant Jones of 1 Troop, 14 Field Squadron, Royal Engineers, following in a

Sergeant Peter Robinson DCM.

172

light armoured car, was to start defusing the demolition charges that were known to litter the bridge's structure. Lord Carrington was to follow in his squadron headquarters tank. The orders group ended with Major Trotter formally shaking hands with Sergeant Robinson and reassuringly saying 'Don't worry, I'll let your wife know, if you don't come back.' Having seen the fate of the two troops who had earlier attempted to move onto the Kaiser Lodewijk Plein, it seemed more than likely that Major Trotter would have to deliver this message.

According to Sergeant Robinson's Army issue wristwatch, the first move forward started at 18.13 hours. Peter Carrington noted that 'It was not quite dark, as we went over'. Nosing forward across the Kaiser Lodewijk Plein, Sergeant Robinson's tank was engaged by an 88mm but the hasty shot ricocheted off the road and struck the Sherman a glancing blow, disabling the vital radio set. While his troop commander withdrew under smoke, Lance Sergeant Billingham became the 88mm's target but the troop's other two tanks were stationary and ready to give covering fire. Sergeant Pacey engaged the 88mm with HE and reduced the German gun to scrap before Sergeant Billingham was hit.

Back in cover, the troop reorganised, with Sergeant Robinson moving to a tank with a working radio. Under pressure from the Commanding Officer's repeated orders to get going, the Shermans were moving forward again into the enemy's killing area on the approaches to the bridge. The ramp was covered by three enemy anti-tank guns and numerous *Panzerfausts*. At about 19.00 hours, driven forward by admirable self-

A Guardsman and a paratrooper inspect a knocked out German 88 on the edge of the Kaiser Lodewijk Plein.

discipline and three hundred years of regimental tradition, Sergeant Robinson recalls how:

'We had barely travelled fifty yards, when a Panzerfaust

struck a nearby girder. It seemed that projectiles were coming from every angle, yet strangely we remained intact. Not only was the bridge defended from both flank and front, but we suffered repeated attacks from the air in the form of men hanging from girders dropping grenades, while snipers endeavoured to keep us running blind [by keeping the Sergeant closed down in his turret].'

The tanks commanded by Sergeant Robinson and Lance Sergeant Pacey charged over the bridge, engines roaring, with their Browning machine-guns firing. As they crossed the vast structure, Germans shot in the bridge's girders plummeted to the roadway below or hung grotesquely from safety straps as their lifeblood ebbed away. These were not suicide snipers but mainly SS engineers working on the Bridge checking and repairing the demolition circuits. There has been much discussion about whether or not resistance fighter Jan Van Hoof had cut the demolition circuits but the greatest sin a military engineer can commit is to have his demolition charges fail. They constantly check their multiple electronic circuits and promptly repair any breaks. However, engineers on the bridge, as SS soldiers, were expected to fight determinedly to the last. Some one hundred and eighty German dead were subsequently recovered from the bridge and its structure. Many more would have fallen into the river below. From his forward observation post on the riverbank, to the east of the bridge, SS-*Brigadeführer* Harmel, in the twilight, only had glimpses of the smoke shrouded bridge. He recalls how:

'*Model had told Bittrich that the Nijmegen Waal bridges were not to be destroyed but the bridges were still prepared for demolition. As the crisis came, I watched from the bunker on the riverbank. When I lost radio to Euling, I knew that the bridge was going to be taken. Everything seemed to pass through my mind all at once. What must be done first? What was the most important action to take? It all came down to the bridges. They must be destroyed. If Bittrich had been in my shoes, he would have blown the main bridge. In my view, Model's order was now cancelled because the situation had changed. I had no intention of being arrested and shot by Berlin for letting the Bridges fall into enemy hands – no matter how Model felt about it.*

I waited, watching and then saw one tank on the centre of the bridge, then another following behind and to a side. I ordered the

The bunker where Heinz Harmel watched the Grenadier tanks cross the bridge. From here he gave the order to blow the demolition charges.

pioneer with the firing mechanism to "Get ready" and when two more tanks reached the centre, I gave the order, on my own responsibility "Let it blow!" Nothing happened. "Again" I shouted to the pioneer. I waited to see the bridge collapse with the tanks into the river. It failed to go up – probably because the initiation cable had been cut by artillery fire. Instead, the tanks kept moving forward getting bigger and closer. "My God, they'll be here in two minutes", I told my radio operator.'

The leading tanks raced on across the long exposed bridge, under fire all the way and skidded sideways, at speed, through a concrete chicane roadblock at the northern end. Against all the odds, they were across! Almost immediately Guardsman Lesley Johnson, Sergeant Robinson's gunner, spotted the first of a pair of anti-tank guns on the bridge's ramp fifty metres away and

The concrete chicane road block on the Lent end of the Bridge and flak tower.

knocked it out with his third round of HE. The tank charged on brushing aside the second enemy gun and grinding the bodies of the crew under the tracks as it passed. Such was Johnson's surprise at surviving the 'running of the gauntlet of fire' that he declared that: 'I swear to this day that Jesus Christ rode on the front of our tank'.

Immediately behind Sergeant Robinson's troop, was Lieutenant Jones of the Royal Engineers in his scout car with orders to make the bridge's demolition charges safe. He recalls:

'I tried, with binoculars, to see if there were any demolition charges, but there were none visible. I left the house and went up behind the forwarCompany D to see how close they had got to the bridge. They had just lost their company commander in addition to a lot of men and were in no condition to push on much further, so I decided to go back. When I got back to my car at about 18.00 hours, I found an urgent order from OC 14 Field Squadron to report to the roundabout near the bridge at once. I arrived at 18.20 hours and found a troop of 2/Grenadier Guards tanks lined up ready to rush the bridge at once...

On the bridge, the first thing I saw was about half a dozen wires on the footway at the side of the bridge. These I cut. I walked up to the roadblock and saw about ten Tellermine in a slit trench nearby. These were obviously designed to close the block. ... I removed the igniters and threw them in the river.'

Lieutenant Tony Jones.

Lieutenant Jones with his scout car covering him made his way back towards Nijmegen checking as he went. He found no more obviously dangerous cables or charges, as the Germans had camouflaged them by building them into the bridges structure. He did, however, collect prisoners and returning to the Nijmegen end of the bridge he,

'handed the seven men over to the CO and reported that, in my opinion, the bridge was safe and all that was now necessary was a detailed search.'

Lieutenant Jones led his troop onto the bridge along with a German POW who agreed to help his captors:

'He led us to the next pier, [at the northern end of the

176

second span]... *There was an elaborate system of staging and the charges were made of TNT packed in green painted boxes, each charge with a serial number corresponding to a serial number painted on the girder. The charges were to be fired electrically, and the detonators were in and connected to one of the wires, which I had previously cut on the deck. We removed these and decided to check the rest of the bridge, though our prisoner had said there were no more charges.'*

It would seem that the bridge was not comprehensively prepared for demolition and that the charges found by Lieutenant Jones were placed, in the time available, with the aim of blowing a single span. However, by following on behind the Grenadier's tanks and quickly cutting the cables, Lieutenant Jones thwarted SS-*Brigadeführer* Harmel's self-appointed mission to blow the bridge. Luck, on this occasion, had been on the side of the Allies. Without capturing the Road Bridge intact, there would have been no chance of XXX Corps reaching the Rhine and in this case, the fate of the battle rested in one man's hands – Lieutenant Tony Jones of the Royal Engineers.

Turn around, drive back and pass under the Bridge. Park opposite the

British engineers, collect up wiring and explosives that were intended to blow the bridge. Note the numbered demolition charges.

steps up the embankment to the main Arnhem road.

On the northern bank, after their assault crossing and maddened charge against the German positions on the dyke, 504 PIR's paratroopers fanned out in small groups, as during the assault their ranks had been greatly thinned. Leading a group of no more than fifteen men towards the bridges was Captain Moffatt Burriss, commander of Company I, who recalls:

'At sundown, we found ourselves under the massive Nijmegen Bridge, which rose nearly twenty stories. The dyke road ran under the north end of the bridge, which was supported by huge concrete columns. An eerie silence had fallen at the north end, and we didn't see any enemy troops. Across the river, the city of Nijmegen was ablaze, and there was a great deal of firing around the bridge's south end.

As I stood beneath the north end, I saw a set of concrete steps that went from the lower road to the main highway at that end. ... Then I turned to La Riviere and pointed up the concrete stairway. "Let's go up!" As I reached the top of the steps, I saw a lone Kraut standing at the end of the bridge. He was so surprised to see us that he dropped his rifle, held up his arms, and immediately surrendered.

The northern end of the Nijmegen bridge and the steps that Moffatt Buriss climbed to meet Sergeant Robinson and Captain the Lord Carrington.

La Riviere and an enlisted man were standing with me at the end of the bridge. I had just told La Riviere to take some men, start across the bridge, and cut wires, when a German hiding

high in the girders shot and killed the enlisted man standing between us. La Riviere immediately wheeled around and shot the Kraut. As the man fell, one of his straps caught in the girders, and he was caught in the steel structure. When we left two days later, he was still hanging there.

It was beginning to get dark. As we looked at the south end of the bridge, we saw silhouettes of tanks heading across in our direction. We couldn't tell if they were German or British, but I think most of us believed that they were Kraut reinforcements. "Let's get off the bridge and over the embankment," I said, "until we can tell whose they are."

As we waited with Gammon grenades in our hands, two tanks passed within a few feet of us. They were British. When the third one arrived, we swarmed all over it and shouted, "Hey, we're Americans!" The tank commander stuck out his head. I grabbed him around the neck. "You guys are the most beautiful sight I have seen in months".'

Captain Lord Carrington remembers this meeting. However, as they were exchanging relieved greetings, the sound of battle could be heard ahead in Lent, on the road to Arnhem.

Two dead SS engineers lying dead on the Nijmegen bridge. Some one hundred and eighty Germans were killed in an attempt to hold it.

Vehicles of Guards Armoured Division cross the road bridge over the Waal at Nijmegen.

The question of who captured the bridges has understandably exercised members of the two divisions and many commentators. However, almost sixty years after the event, it can be said that the capture of the bridge was a joint operation and a joint success. As General Gavin estimated, it would almost certainly have taken the Allies much longer to fight their way to the bridges without the truly heroic Waal crossing by 3/504 PIR. It should also be born in mind, that capturing just one end of the equally large bridge at Arnhem hardly constituted securing a viable crossing. On this basis, honours at Nijmegen are shared equally between the Guards and the 82nd Airborne. On meeting General Gavin for the first time, several days after the bridges' capture, General Dempsey did say,

'I am proud to meet the commanding general of the finest division in the world today.'

In General Gavin's words:

'... I accepted it with reservations, believing that he was being too kind. However, an alert staff officer overheard the comment, and it became part of the division's history.'

If the question of who captured the bridge is easily settled, the issue of the lack of immediate exploitation of the success can not be so easily settled and is a source of enduring controversary.

CHAPTER NINE

LENT – NORTH OF THE WAAL

Night Wednesday 20 / Thursday 21 September 1944

Do not take the ramp up to the main Arnhem road but follow the local road (**Griftdijk Sud**) at the foot of the embankment, towards **Elst**, that runs parallel to the highway. Follow the road through Lent until the railway underpass is reached.

Five tanks had set out across the bridge. Sergeants Robinson and Pacey, with the benefit of surprise, got across and continued on into Lent. Guardsman Johnson recalls how Robinson was shouting into his radio's microphone:

Aerial photograph of the two bridges taken 10 September 1944.

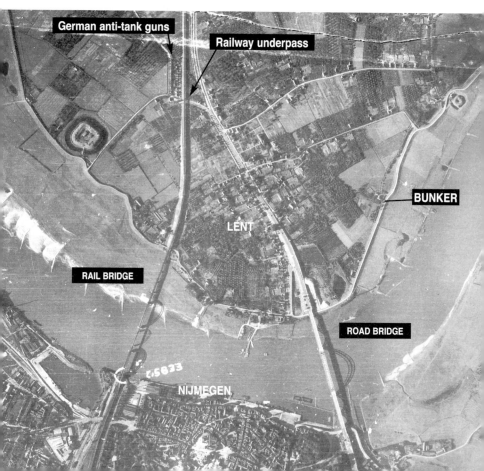

'He had a voice like a bull and that, I think, annoyed me more than anything. It was coming through my earphones like claps of thunder'.

The Troop's other two tanks were hit by a hail of solid, armour piercing shot and *Panzerfausts*, on the northern ramp and one had caught fire. Sergeant 'Rockey' Knight's tank collided with the vehicle in front of him that had been hit by the SS infantry who were still in the area in considerable numbers. He recalls:

'We were fired at. Everybody jumped from the tank and I hit the slope of the causeway beside the tank. After a while a German kicked me and apparently fancied me dead. On closer inspection of our tank, it was actually the cam nets and luggage that had been set afire on the backside of our tank on top of the motor compartment. I re-entered the tank – nobody inside – and managed to drive it in the direction the others had gone. I didn't see any of my crew members. Afterwards I learned they had been made POW.'

One of those taken prisoner, Ernie Wheateley, recalls:

'I jumped into a Jerry foxhole out of the way. Hearing somebody walking about overhead about ten minutes later, I took a look and there was an awful looking Jerry peering down at me, to say, "Come out Tommy", which I promptly did, having no Sten or other gun with which to defend myself. He says, "Where are your mates?" and before I could say anything, out they came.'

Word went out that Sergeant Knight's vital tank needed a crew. Forward stepped some intrepid paratroopers, who in previous service, had crewed Shermans. For the remainder of the night one of the Grenadiers' tanks, was crewed by British and American soldiers.

Meanwhile, Sergeant Robinson's two leading Shermans, exposed on the roadway surrounded by the buildings of Lent, had run a gauntlet of *Panzerfaust* fire. As they headed north, they had a brush with another group of Americans. Captain Burriss recounts how:

'We later learned that the tank commanded by British Sergeant Robinson encountered some troops in a ditch just ahead of him. Thinking they were Germans, he fired on them. One tossed a Gammon grenade back at him. They both realized their mistake and, because no one had been hurt, they held a brief celebration.'

Having driven off the bridge's ramp towards Lent the next problem encountered was an enemy *Sturmguschutz*. Lying in wait, it got off the first shot but missed. While the German gunners were reloading, Guardsman Lesley Johnson laid the sight of his 75-mm gun on the bulk of the enemy vehicle and fired.

'"Target!" I shouted, as I saw the flash of steel striking steel but we wanted to make sure and pumped several more rounds into the hulk.'

A little further on, in the centre of Lent, the church was 'swarming with Germans' who were surprised by the unexpected arrival of British tanks. The enemy infantry were driven into the building by the Shermans' coaxial machine-gun fire. Sergeant Robinson ordered Johnson to engage with main armament. The armour piercing round already in the breach crashed through the church walls followed by high explosive rounds, which they kept firing until the church was ablaze. The surprised SS infantry broke under the hail of the Grenadiers' fire and as they ran, illuminated by the fiercely burning church, the two tanks fired down the village street. Guardsman Johnson wryly pointed out that Sergeant Robinson's motto had been 'If it moves shoot it!' and they did a lot of shooting at moving targets in Lent.

Sergeant Robinson's two tanks continued in the dark, on through Lent to where the railway bridge crosses the wide tree lined concrete road from the northern end of the bridge. Reaching the railway bridge, the Grenadiers' Shermans cautiously went under it and on towards Arnhem. Guardsman Johnson, who admits to having been 'gripped with the cold

The railway bridge at the northern end of Lent. Two of the Grenadiers' tanks went under the bridge just after dark on 20 September 1944.

Coming under the rail bridge and swinging around this bend, Sergent Robinson came under fire from a German anti-tank gun.

hand of battle' at the time, wrote:

'We went round at 15 M.P.H., machine-gunning as we went. Suddenly there were two terrific explosions right in front of the tank. The blast from them came down the periscope and into my eyes and I thought for a minute that I had been blinded.'

The Guardsmens' luck had run out. They had met a roadblock created by two mutually supporting German anti-tank guns. In the now complete darkness, it was impossible to tell exactly where they were and unable to deploy off the road and without infantry they could make no further progress. Withdrawing the two tanks back behind the railway line Sergeant Robinson saw:

'One American paratrooper who I beckoned over, and then from nowhere there suddenly appeared thirty of his comrades, who gave me a most royal welcome, climbing all over my tank. It was the first time I had ever seen a tank kissed, whilst frankly, I felt like kissing them.'

Both paratroopers and armour were pleased to have the mutual support of one another but there was no serious discussion about continuing the advance. The Americans were very low on ammunition and even if the two tanks had got past the anti-tank guns that were blocking the road ahead, the gauntlet of *Panzerfausts* would certainly have claimed them long before they reached Arnhem. The real factor was, however, human. Both the British and American soldiers had been through, by any military measure, traumatic events in the preceding hours

184

and had understandably run out of drive and the 'pot of courage' was drying rapidly.

Captain Lord Carrington had crossed the bridge sometime after Sergeant Robinson's troop and, as we have seen, met up with Captain Moffatt Burriss who had arrived at the northern end of the bridge. The cordiality of the initial meeting was quickly lost, when the three tanks who had gone forward to Lent returned to the area of the northern end of the Bridge's ramp. Captain Burriss recalls:

'That's when the British tank crews brought out their teapots. I was furious. I charged to the front of the tank line, where I found the British commander Captain Peter Carrington of the Grenadier Guards. "Why are you stopping." I asked him. "I can't proceed," he said crisply. "That gun will knock out my tanks." "We will go with you. We can knock out that gun." After crossing the river in those flimsy boats, taking out the machine-guns, knocking out the Germans' 20-mm gun, and capturing the bridge, I had no doubt that we could handle the German 88. "I can't go on without orders." He was a British captain and I was an American captain. He wasn't about to recognize my authority. "No," he said, "I have to have orders from my British commander." I could not believe what I was hearing. "You mean to tell me you're going to sit here on your ass while your own British paratroopers are being cut to shreds – and all because of only one gun?" He shook his head. "I can't go without orders." I looked him straight in the eye. "You yellow son of a bitch. I've just sacrificed half of my company in the face of dozens of guns, and you won't move because of one gun." Then I cocked my Tommy gun, put it up to his head, and said "You get this tank moving, or I'll blow your damn head off." With that he ducked into his tank and locked the hatch. I couldn't get to him.

About half an hour later, Major Cook [commanding 3/504 PIR] had a similar argument with him but to no avail. And an hour or so after that, Colonel Tucker [commanding 504 PIR] had the same argument. He told Carrington, "Your boys are hurting up there at Arnhem. You'd better go. Its only eleven miles." Still no movement. ... In retrospect, we were probably too hard on Carrington. He had little option but to wait for orders; however, we took out our anger on him because the man responsible was nowhere in sight.'

185

Lieutenant Pitt whose platoon remained in close defence of the recalls how:

'By the time we got there, Cook, who was the Battalion Commander was there. And then, the first British tanks came roaring across the bridge. Most of H Company and G Company came shortly afterwards. I don't know how many of them. Then came a couple of jeeps and [General] Gavin and his radioman. By then, it was practically dark, along came a staff car, and out got the British commander. He was, I guess, the corps commander. I'm not sure who he was. Gavin said "We will put some men up on the tanks and in front of the tanks and lets head for Arnhem." I think it was some ten miles or so – it wasn't far. This British commander said "We don't move our tanks at night." Gavin said "You don't move them at night? Well if we wait till daylight then they [the Germans] will move some stuff in." The Brit said "Well, we can't move tanks at night." Gavin said "If they were my men in Arnhem we would move tanks at night. We would move anything at night to get there." This guy said "We are not. We will move them in the morning."'

Captain Burriss's 'man responsible' had many factors to consider on the night of 20/21 September 1944 and the situation was far from straightforward. Firstly, during the course of 20 September ten miles of the 82nd Airborne's rear south-east perimeter from Beek to Molenhoek was under heavy attack and had sucked in all available reserves. The 82nd's divisional reserve, the Coldstream Guards Group, had been deployed to Molenhoek in the afternoon to blunt an attack that threatened the vital Heumen Bridge. Secondly, for much of the day, Hell's Highway had been cut in the area of Son by 107th Panzer Brigade. This very badly delayed the delivery of combat supplies, the lifeblood of an armoured division, as well as further combat troops. Thirdly, following the expenditure of virtually all their ammunition in covering the 3/504's crossing of the Waal, XXX Corps' artillery and the Irish Guards ammunition was so low that they were in no position to continue the attack. Fourthly, the battle in Nijmegen was still going on, with determined SS soldiers adding considerable confusion to attempts to consolidate and reorganize. Finally, at 19.30 hours information, as recorded in both 504 PIR's and 82nd Airborne's signal log records,

'South east of Arnhem: three Tiger tanks, two companies of

infantry and a heavy gun are on their way to Lent/Nijmegen.'
Surely, this information shaped the decision made that evening not to commit the few Shermans available. These practical difficulties created significant problems for the Allied commanders and prevented them from mounting an immediate advance to Arnhem.

To put XXX Corps difficulties in a wider context, two other views complete the debate. Firstly, Major Geoffrey Powell, who was defending a sector of 1st Airborne Division's perimeter at Oosterbeek, commented about the Guards' failure to advance on the night of the 20/21 September 1944:

> *'And so the Grenadiers did, as the Irish had done during the breakout from the Meuse-Escaut Canal [stop over night]. However, to some of the airborne officers, both British and American, who watched the Guards at work, they did give the impression of being deliberate and unflappable, as Guardsmen are expected to be, but possibly rather too much so at times.'*

The implication of this is that the prospect of an early end to the war was effecting the British ground troops performance in battle; much as it effected the 1st Airborne Division's desire to get into battle in the 'final days of the war'. Secondly, General Gavin's airborne view:

> *'I cannot tell you the anger and bitterness of my men. I found Tucker at dawn so irate that he was almost unable to speak. There is no soldier in the world that I admire more than the British, but British infantry leaders somehow did not understand the camaraderie of the airborne troops. To our men there was only one objective: to save their brother paratroopers in Arnhem.'*

Or as Captain Moffatt Burriss said in a more direct and soldierly

German PAK 75mm anti-tank gun.

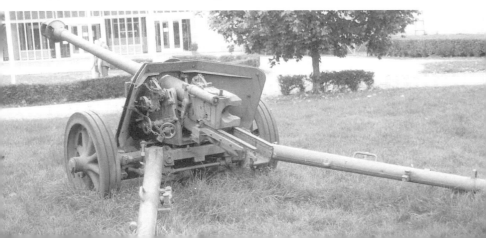

manner over fifty years after the event:

'I am not a profane man but we busted our arses to get across that river so they could get to our airborne brothers. Why didn't they move?'

However, Lieutenant General Horrocks's case is compelling in its simple military analysis. He summed up the situation as follows:

'The forward troops always think that those in the rear are leading a life of ease and should be doing more, but even Jim Gavin, the divisional commander, could have had no idea of the utter confusion which reigned in Nijmegen at the time with sporadic battles going on all over the place, and particularly on our one road to the rear where chaos reigned. [Ahead] was infantry country, and realizing this, I had ordered up the 43rd Wessex Division to move through Nijmegen and launch a divisional attack towards Arnhem. I did not realize at this time that they also were badly blocked on that one "blasted" road which was constantly under fire and so often cut. ... As regards the troops immediately available, the Irish Guards Infantry were reduced to five platoons [probably more].

'I now began to feel as though I was in a boxing ring, fighting a tough opponent with one arm tied behind my back. I was in fact, trying to fight three battles at the same time. The first was to keep open my tenuous supply line, which stretched back along one road for over fifty miles to Eindhoven and beyond; much of which was being frequently cut by an increasing number of German forces operating on both sides of this single road link. The second battle was to prevent the Germans closing in on Nijmegen itself, especially from the wooded country to the east of the town. Finally, I was desperately trying to force a way through to the north bank of the Neder Rhijn to join up with the embattled parachute troops.'

At the time, those fighting at Nijmegen did not know that 2/Para's tenuous hold on the Arnhem Bridge's northern ramp was finally lost during the afternoon of Wednesday 20 September, some three hours before the Nijmegen Bridges were seized. They had heroically held their positions with a battalion strength group for sixty-eight hours, which was twenty hours longer than Montgomery had required, but fell short of the seventy-two hours promised by General Urquhart. If all of 1st Parachute Brigade had been able to reach the Arnhem Bridge, let alone the rest of the division, may be the hopelessly over optimistic timings facing XXX Corps and the US airborne divisions would not have mattered. This is, of course, only one of the campaign's major 'what if' questions.

German emergency ferry at Pannerden.

In response to the changed situation, SS-*Brigadeführer* Harmel demanded greater efforts from his SS engineers. The vital panzer sub units were crossing the Pannerden Ferry by last light on 20 September and heading towards Lent. Harmel recalled that:

> 'Ferrying across the Pannerdensh Canal was very slow for the first days. When we started, we could transport only men and light vehicles and then my Division's remaining *Sturmgeschütz*. It took my engineers more than two days [PM 20 September] to build a raft to take the panzers that were then arriving from the factories in the Reich. I myself had crossed the ferry with my tactical headquarters and set up at Doorenburg.'

Even if the Allies had the combat power to drive on towards Arnhem on the night of 20/21 September, they would have been unable to deploy off the road. In addition, as Sergeant Robinson found, they would have been under fire from the uncleared flanks, such as the fortified enemy position at Oosterhout. In addition, Harmel had directed that all available units were,

> 'to block the road between Elst and Lent with every available anti-tank gun and artillery piece because if we don't they'll roll straight through to Arnhem'.

Nijmegen bridge from the Nijmegen side in Spring 1945.

If the Guards had been able to advance, the resulting encounter battle would have brought the advance to a halt with heavy tank losses. The opportunity to complete the MARKET GARDEN plan had long since passed with the failure to seize the Nijmegen Bridges at the beginning of the battle.

Final Thoughts

Let the words of Captain Moffatt Burriss sum up the climax of the battle for the Nijmegen Bridges at the tactical level:

> *'The 3rd Battalion, 504, had accomplished the impossible. We had crossed the Waal. We had attacked across two miles of heavily defended open terrain. We had seized the two vital Nijmegen Bridges. We had opened the lifeline to Arnhem. And it had cost the Krauts plenty.'*

However, that lifeline was too late coming for 2/PARA at the Arnhem Bridge. The victor of the MARKET GARDEN campaign, SS-*Brigadeführer* Harmel, has the final word. After nearly fifty years of reflection, he said:

> *'What is seldom understood is that the Arnhem battle was in reality won at Nijmegen. If the Allies had taken the* [Nijmegen] *Bridge on the first day, it would have been all over for us. Even if we had lost it on the second day, we would have had difficulty stopping them. By the time the English tanks arrived, the matter was already decided.'*

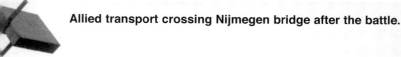

Allied transport crossing Nijmegen bridge after the battle.

OOUSTERHOUT – PRIVATE TOWLE
CONGRESSIONAL MEDAL OF HONOR

Thursday 21 September 1944

Take the turning to the left just after the railway underpass (**Zaligestraat**). This road takes the visitor back to the Waal. Just before the junction is the **Hof van Holland** fort surrounded by trees and a moat. Hof van Holland is now private holiday homes but it is possible to park and have a good look at the moat and bridge that 3/504 PIR attacked across.

Driving on a short distance the **Oosterhout Dijk** road is reached. Cross under the railway bridge, with its pillbox still upon the embankment, and continue on to 3/504 PIR's crossing site. Park by the 82nd's memorial on the bend.

The earning of the 82nd Airborne Division's only Congressional Medal of Honor awarded during the Second World War, took place on the Island on the afternoon of 21 September 1944. 1/504 PIR were holding the left flank of the Waal bridgehead facing Oosterhout. Company C had been keeping groups of German infantry, who had been attempting to advance on them, at bay with well-aimed rifle fire, which accounted for around twenty enemy soldiers. This situation did not last for long. Sergeant Ross S Carter recorded:

'War with a stubborn and resourceful enemy, however, never offers a one-way advantage for long. Our successful rifle fire invited retaliation which came at first as a heavy artillery barrage and, second, in the form of preparations for an attack

82nd Airborne Division's monument, wth a tablet listing all those killed during the action in the Nijmegen area. Included is Private Towle's name along with Congressional Medal of Honor.

with armour. Five Mark VI [Tiger] tanks, supported by numerous infantrymen, moved into the little town and then towards us. Behind the opposite bank of the road, we heard them roaring and clanking. Then we saw five great shapes lined up in assault formation. The long gleaming guns stuck up like vicious snouts of prehistoric monsters almost to the top of the road. Only the high bank prevented them from lowering the muzzles enough to hit us. The Kraut infantry, full of respect for our unerring marksmanship stayed out of sight in the ditches. They were waiting for the kill like jackals.'

These Tigers were a part of Major Knaust's reinforced *Kampfgruppe* that had forced its way through the wreckage on the Arnhem Bridge, south onto the road to Nijmegen. Sergeant Carter continues:

'Since the field behind us was perfectly level and clear back to the river, if the tanks once got over the road we were lost. Now it was only a matter of minutes until they would come, perhaps until most or all of us would be dead. We were conjecturing whether the Krauts would wipe us all out or give us a chance to surrender when slim, youthful Towle, followed by James K carrying some shells, came hurrying up with his bazooka. Towle who had joined us in Italy, was a quiet, self possessed, dark-haired boy whose fate and luck it was to be the only bazooka man in the company with any ammunition.

He climbed up the bank, took a quick peep at the tanks, then slid down and got his bazooka. He said ironically "I see I am going to get the Congressional today." He crawled back up and set to work. He would fire his metal pipe, slide down to reload, then crawl back up to a new point. The Krauts swivelled their 88s and tank machine-guns to cover the different portions of the embankment; wherever he stuck his weapon over, they sniped at him point blank range. Towle was facing five tanks weighing sixty tons each. Three hundred tons of mobile forts were being opposed by one man and one bazooka! Finally the stout-hearted trooper forced the tanks to withdraw to the town. His bravery saved our company and the left bank of the Rhine.

In a few minutes a mortar shell dropped on Towle and killed him. Towle got his Congressional posthumously.'

Born in Cleveland Ohio, the death of Private John R Towle was described in a citation published in a General Order on 15 March 1945:

'Hurriedly replenishing his supply of ammunition, Pvt. Towle, motivated only by his high conception of duty which called for the destruction of the enemy at any cost, then rushed approximately 125 yards through grazing enemy fire to an exposed position from which he could engage the enemy half-track with his rocket launcher. While in a kneeling position preparatory to firing on the enemy vehicle, Pvt. Towle was mortally wounded by a mortar shell. By his heroic tenacity, at the price of his life, Pvt. Towle saved the lives of many of his comrades and was directly instrumental in breaking up the enemy counterattack'.

The Company C's relief was not long lived as the tanks were seen forming up for another attack: Staff Sergeant Carter continues:

'Word came down the line that the Captain had requested British tank support. We looked down the road towards the bridge, hoping doubtfully that the British would come in time, as it was four o'clock. They never passed up teatime to our knowledge. We listened to the tanks growling in the little town

Watched by American paratroopers, Cromwells of the Welsh Guards cross the Nijmegen Bridge.

and for the sound of the British tanks.

At last we heard the enemy tanks start moving. Our hearts plummeted to our boots. Then far down the road we heard a vast roaring. The British were coming. Soon six Cromwell tanks, followed by British infantry came into sight. We hit the bottom of our holes knowing that the enemy would redouble his shellfire. The British tanks came up and set to work in a most matter-of-fact way. They knocked out three Mark VIs almost instantly and machine-gunned everything in sight.

A machine-gun in a big house across the road fired on them. Immediately a tank shot an armour-piercing shell through the house, followed by a white phosphorus shell, which exploded inside. A hullabaloo started within, succeeded in short order by a mass exodus in a mad rush. Next, they blew a mortar position to hell. These helpful actions plus the tac-tac of their machine guns beat the music of gratitude deep into our hearts. They had achieved a Lone Ranger rescue in grand style. Their job done, the gallant tank cavaliers rumbled off the way they had come. Since, however, the hour was well past teatime, they pulled into a nearby wood to have their spot.'

The delayed arrival of the Cromwell tanks of the 2/Welsh Guards at the front near Oosterhout had not been the result 'tea stops'. Sitting in his Sherman's turret, Major Fisher of No. 1 Squadron jotted down his impressions, while stuck behind a battlegroup ahead that had been stopped in its tracks on the road to Arnhem:

'1.0 p.m.   My tank is just crossing the Waal.

1.15 p.m.   We are stationary on the bridge ... it is slightly uncomfortable as we are a perfect, silhouetted target for German bombers, if any.

2 p.m.   This bridge is not attractive ... There is a certain amount of small-arms fire from time to time, but I can't make out quite where from.

2.15 p.m.   When I was out of my tank just now a bullet whistled past my nose – literally. Soon after we had a mortar concentration all round us ... now there are lots of enemy planes over us. One man has been slightly wounded in the squadron. What a bloody place to be sitting!

2.45 p.m.   More planes over us quite low. This is an unpleasant situation I shall not forget this bridge for a long time.

3.15 p.m.   More shelling and mortaring. Brigade, Division

The King with Generals Horrocks and Gavin meeting members of the 82nd Airborne after the battle.

and Corps Commanders have all gone forward in succession to make a plan to deal with the opposition. Meanwhile we stay on this dammed bridge.

4.30 p.m.   Mortaring every now and again to keep us worried but nothing as close as before ... I hope we shall not have to stay on this bridge all night.'

However, just after 17.00 hours (well after teatime) they were able to move forward and on to the road around to the left flank of the bridgehead, via Oosterhout. Riding on the tanks were infantrymen of 1/Welsh Guards. Lieutenant MC Devas was commanding the leading troop who 'nosed their way carefully along the winding lane'. In the gathering darkness, they engaged the enemy Tigers with their 17-pounder guns, mounted in the Challenger variants of the standard Cromwell and knocked three of them out, thus more than earning their keep. The Squadron was ordered to pull back, as the Guards

Armoured Division's attempt to beak out to Arnhem was halted on the main route north. However, the Welshmen remained in the wood, in support of 1/504 PIR, prepared to counter the threat of the Tigers against this thinly held sector of the still vulnerable bridgehead.

Despite renewed attempts by 43rd Wessex Division's infantry and tanks of 8 Armoured Brigade on the direct and flanking routes to the banks of the Rhine, XXX Corps were too late to reach the Arnhem bridge. The beleaguered men of 2/PARA were overwhelmed and the remainder of 1st Airborne Division, failing to reach them, were driven back into a defensive perimeter, of no tactical significance, several miles west of the vital bridge. On the night of 25/26 September the British Airborne troops were evacuated. Ever since then, airborne, armoured and infantry commanders and soldiers have wondered if they could have done more to reach 1st Airborne Division. However, others say that the entire MARKET GARDEN concept was 'vainglorious' and that the air, and hence the airborne, plan was fatally flawed. The debate will go on and this acount will be continued in another Battleground Europe volume; *The Island.*

Grenadier Guards give American paratroopers of 82nd Airborne a lift to the fighting in Nijmegen.

APPENDIX I

ORDERS OF BATTLE

XXX BRITISH CORPS

GUARDS ARMOURED DIVISION

NB. The Guards Armoured Division had by September 1944 departed from their official ORBAT to form, uniquely, regimental groups of armour and infantry that habitually fought together. This closeness, unusual at the time, between the two arms brought many benefits. However, their critics, with little solid evidence, also use this grouping to attribute 'a certain ponderousness' to the Division.

HQ GUARDS ARMOURED DIVISION
  Guards Armoured Division Signal Regiment (-)

HQ 5th GUARDS ARMOURED BRIGADE ('Group Hot')
  1st (Motorized) Battalion, The Grenadier Guards
  2nd (Armoured) Battalion, The Grenadier Guards
  1st (Armoured) Battalion, The Coldstream Guards
  5th Battalion, The Coldstream Guards
  55th Field Regiment Royal Artillery
  14th Field Squadron Royal Engineers

HQ 32nd GUARDS ARMOURED BRIGADE ('Group Cold')
  2nd (Armoured) Battalion, The Irish Guards
  3rd Battalion, The Irish Guards
  1st Battalion, The Welsh Guards
  2nd (Armoured Recconnisance) Battalion, The Welsh Guards
  153rd (Leicestershire Yeomanry) Field Regiment Royal Artillery
  615th Field Squadron Royal Engineers

GUARDS ARMOURED DIVISIONAL TROOPS
  HQ 21st Anti-Tank Regiment Royal Artillery
  HQ 94th Light Anti-Aircraft Regiment Royal Artillery

HQ Guards Armoured Division Engineer Regiment,
Field Park Company, 11th Bridging Troop RE
and Divisional Postal Unit
Number 1 Independent Machine-gun Company, The
Royal Northumberland Fusiliers
Royal Army Service Corps
HQ Guards Armoured Division RASC Battalion, and
Tank Delivery Squadron
Royal Army Medical Corps   19th Light Field
Ambulance, 128th Field Ambulance and Field
Hygiene Section
Royal Army Ordnance Corps Guards Armoured
Division Ordnance Field Park, Company
RAOC and Mobile Bath Unit
Royal Electrical and Mechanical Engineers 5th
Guards Armoured Brigade Workshop, 32nd
Guards Armoured Brigade Workshop
Military Police Guards Armoured Division Company
Royal Corps of Military Police
Intelligence Corps Field Security Section

8th INDEPENDENT ARMOURED BRIGADE
4th / 7th Royal Dragoons Guards
13th / 18th Royal Hussars
Nottinghamshire (Sherwood Rangers) Yeomanry
12th Battalion, King's Royal Rifle Corps
147th (Essex Yeomanry) Field Regiment Royal Artillery
(Self Propelled) Anti-Tank Battery Royal Artillery
8th Armoured Brigade Signal Squadron
8th Armoured Brigade Workshop REME
8th Armoured Brigade Ordnance Field Park
552nd Company Royal Army Service Corps
168th (City of London) Light Field Ambulance RAMC
265th Forward Delivery Squadron RAC

ROYAL NETHERLANDS BRIGADE 'PRINCESS IRENE'

147 (Essex Yeomanry) Field Regiment RA in Nijmegen.

21st ARMY GROUP TROOPS (from Army Groups Royal
    Artillery to XXX Corps)
    64th Medium Regiment Royal Artillery (3.5 inch guns)
    419th Heavy Battery (155mm guns)

FIRST ALLIED AIRBORNE ARMY

BRITISH AIRBORNE CORPS

HEADQUARTERS 82nd AIRBORNE DIVISION
    82nd Signal Company and 82nd Headquarter
      Company

    504th PARACHUTE INFANTRY REGIMENT
    1st Battalion, 504th Parachute Infantry Regiment
    2nd Battalion, 504th Parachute Infantry Regiment
    3rd Battalion, 504th Parachute Infantry Regiment

    505th PARACHUTE INFANTRY REGIMENT
    1st Battalion, 505th Parachute Infantry Regiment
    2nd Battalion, 505th Parachute Infantry Regiment
    3rd Battalion, 505th Parachute Infantry Regiment

508th PARACHUTE INFANTRY REGIMENT
1st Battalion, 508th Parachute Infantry Regiment
2nd Battalion, 508th Parachute Infantry Regiment
3rd Battalion, 508th Parachute Infantry Regiment

325th GLIDER INFANTRY REGIMENT
1st Battalion, 325th Glider Infantry Regiment
2nd Battalion, 325th Glider Infantry Regiment
3rd Battalion, 325th (formerly 401st) Glider Infantry Regiment

DIVISIONAL TROOPS
82nd Parachute Maintenance Battalion
307th Airborne Engineer Battalion
307th Airborne Medical Company
80th Airborne Antiaircraft Battalion
319th Glider Field Artillery Battalion
320th Glider Field Artillery Battalion
376th Parachute Field Artillery Battalion
456th Glider Field Artillery Battalion
782nd Ordnance Company
407th Quartermaster Company
666th Quartermaster Truck Company
82nd Military Police Platoon
82nd Reconnaissance Platoon

The German MP 38/40 Sub machine-gun was arguably the most effective weapon of its class ever produced.

German side-arms. The Luger was privately purchased (right) by many officers in preference to the P38 Walther (above).

APPENDIX II

CEMETERIES

'At the going down of the sun
and in the morning,
we will remember them.'

For the Fallen

The MARKET GARDEN Graves

The soldiers of all nations who took part in MARKET GARDEN and were killed in action or died of wounds are now widely spread across Europe, Britain and the USA. However, a significant number still lie in cemeteries on or near the battlefields covered by this book. This appendix contains details of the cemeteries and how to find them.

The Commonwealth War Graves Commission (CWGC)

The Commonwealth War Commission was formed in 1917, originally as the Imperial War Graves Commission, under Major General Sir Fabian Ware. As commander of a Red Cross mobile unit Ware started to record names and locations of grave, which at the time, beyond a wooden cross went largely unrecorded despite Army regulations. Good intentions, however, broke down in the chaos and under the weight of casualties. Under pressure from home the War Office approved the formation of a Graves Registration Unit in 1915, under Ware, who became a Temporary Major. Gradually the importance of the care of war graves grew and in 1917 the present organization was founded. Today the Commission woks in 140 countries and tends 1,146,105 graves and maintains memorials to many thousands more Commonwealth Soldiers who lost their lives in the Twentieth Century.

General Haig commented in 1915:

'It is recognized that the work of the organization is of purely sentimental value, and that it does not directly contribute to the successful termination of the war. It has, however, an extraordinary moral value to the troops as well as to the relatives and friends of the dead at home... Further, on the termination of hostilities, the nation will demand an account from the government as to the steps which have been taken to mark and classify the burial places of the dead...'

CWGC Cemetery Mook

Located on the Mook to Groesbeek road, this cemetery contains 322 graves dating mainly from the fighting in the immediate area during September and October 1944 and from the battles just across the

201

German frontier fought during February 1945. Two hundred and seventy six are British, three are Canadians. Also buried here are soldiers of the 43rd Wessex Division who died on the Island and were originally buried in the US Temporary Cemetery at Molenhoek (See below for details). Amongst the British graves lie eleven Poles with slightly more pointed gravestones. They were killed in the fighting for the Rhineland in 1945.

CWGC Canadian Cemetery and Memorial Wall Groesbeek

This Cemetery is located on Zevenheuvveleweg on the way from Groesbeek to Berg en Dal. The green and white CWGC signs can be picked up from the northern edge of Groesbeek (near the Bevrijdigsmuseum) and from the Wylerban (near the DZ T Memorial). This cemetery dates from the Operation VERITABLE period of early 1945 and, as the cemetery's name suggests, the dead, some 2,338 of them came from Canada. There are also 268 British graves. Most were killed in Germany and this is a rare example of Commonwealth bodies being re-interred in a second country. This was the result of an order by Canadian General Crerar ordering that none of his countrymen were to lie in Germany. Of greater interest to those following Operation MARKET GARDEN, are the two colonnades containing black stone tablets with 1,103 names engraved on them. These tablets are the names of those British, Canadian and South African soldiers killed during the advance from France into Holland and this, of course, includes those who fought in Operation MARKET GARDEN. Clearly, some of the names belong to the unknown graves in the cemetery. There are two VC holders commemorated amongst the names on the memorial. These include those of Lance Sergeant Baskeyfield VC, S Staffs, who fought with 1st Airborne Division in Arnhem and of Sgt Cosens VC, QOR of Canada. The cemetery is still open and receives bodies that are still being discovered in Holland.

CWGC Nijmegen Jonkerbos Cemetery

This cemetery is not easy to find from the direction of Groesbeek. The CWGC signing is somewhat misleading, not to say incomplete! The military cemetery should not be confused with the civilian Jonkerbos

Cemetery. The military cemetery is located on OudeMollenhutseweg just south of the Stadspark. From the Keizer Karel Plein take the Malden, Molenhoek Mook road (Saint Annasraat). Three hundred metres after crossing a bridge over the railway, fork right onto Hatertseweg. The cemetery is approximately six hundred yards on the left. There are 1,460 burials mainly from the MARKET GARDEN period.

American Battle Monuments Commission (ABMC)

Similar to the Commonwealth War Graves Commission, the American Battle Monuments Commission is an agency of the Executive Branch of the US Federal Government. It is responsible for commemorating the service of US Forces world wide since April 1917 (their entry into World War I) by establishing suitable memorials and constructing, operating and maintaining permanent American military cemeteries overseas. The ABMC is also responsible for controlling the design and construction of U.S. military monuments and markers in foreign countries erected by other US citizens and organizations, both public and private; and overseeing their maintenance.

Jonkerbos CWGC Cemetery contains British servicemen killed mainly in the MARKET GARDEN operation.

In 1947, the US Congress decided to give next of kin the option to choose where they would like the serviceman to be buried (unlike the Commonwealth next of kin). The choices were to remain in the theatre where they died or to return them to the US for burial in National Military Cemeteries or under private arrangements in hometown cemeteries. About 63% of all bodies were repatriated during 1948 and 1949. The remaining US military graves were concentrated into a few large cemeteries. Of the 320,423 Second World War bodies of US servicemen, the ABMC is responsible for 93,242 graves across the world. The remainder of the bodies were returned to their families. Also commemorated by the ABMC are the names of 78,976 soldiers who are listed as Missing in Action.

Former US Cemetery at Molenhoek

US Temporary Cemetery 4655 was located in a field behind what used to be the Van de Broek Brewery, which has now been converted into a place of entertainment. The cemetery was started on 20 September 1944 and it is here that 836 Americans, who lost their lives in the Groesbeek, Nijmegen and 'Island' battles of autumn 1944 were laid to rest. Also originally buried here were thirty-eight British and three Canadian soldiers. Some of the British dead, belonged to 43rd Wessex Division who had been cleared from the 'Island' when 101st Airborne Division took over positions there in early October 1944. Also, some belong to 5 Duke of Cornwall's Light Infantry who were under command of the American Division and, consequently, their dead were handled by the US system. Today, all that remains of the cemetery is a memorial at the former main gate. Incidentally, the figure of 637 graves recorded on the monument is incorrect and should read 836. In line with US policy, the graves were moved in 1948 to the US Cemetery at Margarten in southern Holland or repatriated to the US. The British and Canadians were reburied in the nearby CWGC Cemetery Mook. The land occupied by the former cemetery has been returned to agriculture.

Margraten Cemetery

Margraten is the only ABMC cemetery in Holland. The dead who were to remain in the care of the ABMC were brought here from temporary cemeteries across Holland, such as that at Mollenhoek at the foot of the Groesbeek heights. The cemetery is situated in the village of Margraten, six miles east of Maastricht near the southernmost point of Holland some two hours drive south of Nijmegen. The cemetery is well signposted.

Margarten's tall memorial tower is clearly visible as the visitor approaches the site, which covers over sixty acres. From the cemetery entrance, the visitor enters the Court of Honour with its pool reflecting the tower. To the right and left, respectively, are the visitors building and a building containing three engraved maps showing the operations conducted by US Forces in 1944 and 1945. Stretching along the side of the Court are the two Walls of the Missing on which are recorded the names of 1,723 who gave their lives in the service of the USA but who rest in unknown graves. At the base of the tower, facing the reflecting pool is a statue representing the grieving mother of her lost son. Beyond the tower, containing the cemetery's chapel is the burial area. Divided into 16 plots the cemetery contains 8,301 graves, with the headstones set in long curves. A wide tree-lined mall leads to the flagstaff.

In the summer, the cemetery is open to visitors daily from 09.00 - 18.00 hours and in the winter from 09.00 to 17.00 hours. Details of the ABMC its work and cemeteries can be found on the Internet on http://www.usabmc.com/index.shtml

German

The German MARKET GARDEN dead are widely spread in cemeteries across the border in Germany or in the only German war cemetery in Holland at Ijsselstijn.

Ijsselstijn German Cemetery

Ijsselstijn German War Cemetery is sited in a remote spot thirty kilometres west of Eindhoven between that city and Venray. Follow the A270 from Eindhoven to Helmond where the road turns into the N270. Continue until the junction with the N277 is reached. IJsseltijn is a kilometre to the south on the N277.

German soldiers who died and were originally buried in Holland between 1940 and 1945, were disinterred after the war and moved from communal or battlefield cemeteries across Holland and concentrated here for reburial. There are 31,511 bodies interned in this cemetery. Amongst the soldiers who lie here, are the approximately 8,000 Germans killed during Operation MARKET GARDEN. Those from II SS Panzer Corps killed in Arnhem and on the Island were originally buried in the SS Heroes Cemetery on the outskirts of Arnhem. This Cemetery, which had a short existence, was laid out during the period between the end of the battle and Arnhem's eventual liberation in April 1945. In line with normal policy, SS ranks have been converted into their Whermacht equivalents on all graves and memorials.

The Mauser Kar 98K rifle was the standard infantry weapon of the German Infantry.

APPENDIX III

SS Ranks and their British and US equivalents			
Waffen SS		**British Army**	**US Army**
SS-*Brigadeführer*		Brigadier	Brigadier General
SS-*Oberführer*		(not applicable)	Senior Colonel
SS-*Standartenführer*		Colonel	Colonel
SS-*Obersturmbannführer*		Lieutenant Colonel	Lieutenant Colonel
SS-*Sturmbannführer*		Major	Major
SS-*Hauptsturmführer*		Captain	Captain
SS-*Obersturmführer*		Lieutenant	1st Lieutenant
SS-*Untersturmführer*		2nd Lieutenant	2nd Lieutenant
SS-*Sturmscharführer*		Regimental Sergeant Major	Sergeant Major
SS-*Hauptscharführer*		Sergeant Major	Master Sergeant
SS-*Oberscharführer*		(not applicable)	Technical Sergeant
SS-*Scharführer*		Colour Sergeant	Staff Sergeant
SS-*Unterscharführer*		Sergeant	Sergeant
SS-*Rottenführer*		Corporal	Corporal
SS-*Sturmmann*		Lance Corporal	(not applicable)
SS-*Oberschütze*		(not applicable)	Private 1st Class
SS-*Mann*		Private	Private

INDEX

208